Into the Light:
Emerging From the 2020 Pandemic

Mary McManus, MSW

"Light is to darkness what love is to fear; in the presence of one the other disappears." – *Marianne Williamson*

To Phil –

From my heart to yours
with love & gratitude

Mary McManus

Other books by Mary McManus, MSW:
Coming Home: A Memoir of Healing, Hope and Possibility
Going the Distance: The Power of Endurance
The Adventures of Runnergirl 1953
Feel the Heal: An Anthology of Poems to Heal Your Life
Hope is a Garden: Poems and Essays from the 2020 Pandemic

Into the Light: Emerging From the 2020 Pandemic published by

Table of Contents:

Dedication and Acknowledgments:

"Into the Light: Emerging From the 2020 Pandemic" is lovingly dedicated to my husband Tom and our twins, Ruth Anne and Autumn. The tapestry of love woven tight in our family helped us to navigate the turbulent times of the pandemic meeting all challenges with humor, unconditional love, and maintaining our connection via the Signal app.

I want to acknowledge and thank:

My husband Tom for his constant support giving me the time and space for my creative process.

David R. Hamilton, Ph.D., and Bernie Siegel, MD, two wonderful teachers I have been blessed to know who have nurtured and supported my journey of healing and transformation. Their wisdom shined a guiding light as we navigated the uncharted waters of a post-pandemic world.

Our wonderful village with whom we share the miles on and off the roads. We support each other through the trials and celebrate resilience, strength and triumphs meeting life's challenges together.

Introduction

As I wrote "Into the Light: Emerging From the 2020 Pandemic" in real time, I was not sure about the arc of the book. There were times when I wasn't sure there would be a book or what its title would be given the peaks and valleys of the pandemic. Would we ever emerge from the pandemic? After appearing on The Cardinal Café podcast at the end of May, 2021, co-hosts Greg Chastain and Ed Siegel expressed hope that I would continue to write poetry and essays as we began to emerge from the 2020 pandemic. "I've been receiving some promptings from Spirit," I said. Yet I wasn't sure if there was a book to write after "Hope is a Garden: Poems and Essays From the 2020 Pandemic." It seemed as though the pandemic would end with vaccinations. We had a new President with an agenda that would bring us out of the economic crisis created during the previous Administration. After the inauguration of President Biden, hopes were high that climate change, racial injustice and a sense of unrest and divisiveness would be eased. Our country and the world could begin to heal.

As vaccination rates increased and infection rates dropped, masks were tossed in the air. We believed that we were emerging from the pandemic. My first working title for this book was, "Into the Light: Emerging From the 2020 Pandemic." By year's end, it became apparent that we were not emerging from the pandemic but learning how to live in a world with a highly contagious virus that, in an unvaccinated person, could result in severe illness or death. I changed the working title to "Into the Light" believing we needed light, hope and optimism more than ever as the agenda for the Biden Administration was quickly sabotaged in Congress. We have had to learn how to be the light in the midst of confusion, uncertainty, darkness and ongoing divisiveness. We have learned how life is fragile. The words, "Don't it always seem to go that you don't know what you've got til it's gone" seemed to be an anthem for the past two and a half years.

Ever since I was given the life changing diagnosis of Post-Polio Syndrome, a progressive neuromuscular disease by Western

---

Medicine Standards, I cultivated an attitude of gratitude. During this year of emerging from the pandemic, it brought finding ways to be in a state of appreciation to a whole new level. In May, as we took off our masks and celebrated the light at the end of the pandemic's tunnel, I imagined myself once again standing on the stage at the Pre-Race Pasta Dinner during Hyannis Marathon Weekend sharing my journey on the road to the Boston Marathon, and how running kept me running mind, body and soul during the pandemic.

At first we thought that the Hyannis Marathon Weekend would not happen in 2022, but in January, on Facebook, I saw that the Race Director announced that it would go on! The Race Director was not a big fan of masks and, like so many was so over the pandemic. There was nothing on the website about protocols for the race. The host hotel for the weekend, The Hyannis Resort and Conference Center, where we always stayed during "Camp Hyannis" aka Hyannis Marathon weekend had strict pandemic guidelines in place with masking and social distancing. Part of the thrill of Hyannis Marathon Weekend was the crush of people making their way through the Expo and reunions with friends we haven't seen since the previous year. After the first two years of attending race weekend, we gave Race Weekend the nickname "Camp Hyannis." Hugs and high fives and "what are you running this year?" filled the lobby as runners arrived with luggage and coolers in tow. On race morning, everyone stood in line at the café. The energy was electric. The cafe closed during the pandemic.

At first I felt depressed that Hyannis Race Weekend was going to happen knowing that Team McManus would choose to forego the experience. Tom and Ruth Anne were training for the Providence Half Marathon and followed a strict training plan. While we all believed that the wave of the pandemic would once again pass, there was no reason to take a risk for an experience that would be dramatically different from what we had known since 2009. Our last Hyannis Marathon Weekend in February of 2020 was the last event we attended before the first wave of the pandemic wreaked havoc in our lives. I focused on feeling deep gratitude for memories made and the many blessings that are found by being in the present moment.

I held tightly onto hope for the future.

During this past year, we have all had to ride the waves of highs and lows making choices based on the best available knowledge we had at the time. Everyone made choices that they assessed were best for themselves and their loved ones. May these poems and essays uplift, inspire and motivate you to view life through a lens of light, love, gratitude, hope, optimism and faith regardless of life's circumstances.

From my heart to yours
In health and wellness
Mary McManus, MSW
September 2022

"Everything can be taken from a man but one thing: the last of the human freedoms-to choose one's attitude in any given set of circumstance - to choose one's own way." ~Victor Frankl

"But my darling, there's no such thing as the light at the end of the tunnel, you must realize that you are the light." ~Anonymous

Fear or Faith

"I choose faith over anxiety, hope over worry and love over fear."
~Anonymous

I have been very quiet about "the vaccine" in social media, except of course for when I went on the news and shared how easy it was to get Tom's appointment using pre-registration through the state. During the interview, I stayed focused on the positive; vaccinations and continued public health safety measures will lead us out of this pandemic. I didn't share the angst I was experiencing about whether or not I would get the vaccine at the time, saying boldly at the end of the interview that I would schedule my appointment after Tom had his second dose. The on-air interview was very brief but we shared with our reporter, Anna what we were looking forward to once we were both vaccinated. I felt a clutch in my stomach because of my intense ambivalence about taking the vaccine. Tom, on the other hand, felt strongly about getting the vaccine. We had many rather heated discussions about it, but I yielded to his wisdom. I honored his feeling of an urgent need to get it. He does most of the chores outside of the house and was not sure when he might be called to go back into the office to work.

There was a question of whether or not I contracted paralytic polio from the vaccine in 1959. While there is absolute assurance that you cannot get the COVID-19 virus from the vaccine, I had many intense feelings swirling around inside of me. I am an intense proponent of the mind/body connection and creating my own reality.

As friends were getting fully vaccinated and Tom had his first dose of the vaccine, I had feelings resurface from lugging around a leg brace, being left out and being left behind. What a dilemma! I was filled with suffering that I was aware was of my own creation.

I prayed and meditated. I made a firm decision that my daughter Ruth Anne and I would NOT get the vaccine. My Facebook newsfeed flooded with joyful fully vaccinated people. Their profile photos had 'frames' touting their fully vaccinated status. A new

—

social phenomenon emerged. There was a new world order of those who were 'in' having been vaccinated, poised and ready to resume life as we once knew it. We were left wondering how we were going to be able to return to the activities we loved without getting vaccinated.

During Friday's meditation, I felt a deep stirring in my soul. I knew we all needed to be vaccinated. Our son's girlfriend Michelle was being vaccinated through her work and she made an appointment for our son Autumn to receive his on 4/22. It was on the news that I would get my appointment after Tom had his 2nd dose even though at the time I was harboring the view that there was no way I would get the vaccine.

I knew it was going to be super easy to get an appointment through MGH Brigham where I had once received primary care. Both Ruth Anne and I received emails from their system through Patient Gateway about eligibility. Tom's primary care is through MGH Brigham and he received his vaccine through their site at Assembly Row. After meditation ended, I asked Ruth Anne if we could reevaluate our thoughts and feelings about the vaccine. We had spent many hours discerning whether or not to get the vaccine that included recalling what "they," the medical establishment said with great authority about each of our diagnoses and prognoses.

Ruth Anne will be volunteering this summer at ReVision Urban Farm and staff at the Farm have already received their vaccines. We went into her Patient Gateway account and updated her status to give her a higher priority as an agriculture worker. I went into my Patient Gateway and scheduled an appointment for April 14th, the day after Tom receives his second dose.

Ruth Anne and I each know the power of the mind/body connection as we have gone through our journeys to health and wellness. I know how my attitude about the vaccine and how I visualize the experience will effect a positive outcome. I dissolved bone spurs, a breast tumor, a lesion on my nose, grown a new gastroc muscle in my left leg and know the power of the mind/body connection. There is a wealth of research available about the power of the mind/body connection.

I know that the only way forward out of the pandemic is for as many people as possible to receive the vaccine which I now call the "shot of wellness." I experience the anticipatory joy of being with friends, experiencing hugs, no longer be concerned about whether someone in my circle tests "positive", traveling, going out to dinner and feeling a sense of freedom when someone asks if I am fully vaccinated.

I may not agree with certain aspects of the medical model, but I do know, deep in my heart that the Divine has a hand in all of this. It would be fool hardy for me to not do all that I can to help end the pandemic.

I choose faith over fear.

Faith

A bird's eye view of adversity
believing is seeing
transform talons of fear with faith
trusting
listening with promptings from Source
deep within heart and soul
a knowing emerges
out of the fog
once bogged down by appearances
letting go
flying high on hope and prayers
every moment
choosing to be
peaceful
One with all that is
In faith
Freedom.

It's April in Boston again. For the second consecutive year, the Boston Marathon will not take place on the 3rd Monday in April. But compared to last year's overwhelming sense of grief and fear, this year has a palpable sense of hope. We couldn't embrace the joys of Spring last year. By contrast, there is a shared joy for sunshine, blue skies, gardens, flowers blooming, birds singing and looking forward to better days.

By the first week in April, there's a wave of enthusiasm among the global running community and the Boston Strong community in anticipation of Marathon Weekend. Runners share their bibs and their fundraising pages while topping off donations and miles; sharing posts about taper madness. We anticipate a reunion with people who we see once a year making plans for meet ups and meals on Boylston Street and at the Expo.

In lieu of people posting about the anticipation of the Boston Marathon, people are sharing the excitement of getting vaccinations or sharing that they have already been vaccinated. Coincidentally, Boston Marathon Race Director Dave McGillivray and his Team at DMSE have set up mass vaccination sites. When he was first interviewed about spearheading the effort for mass vaccination sites, Dave said that this is a marathon not a sprint.

The energy of anticipation for the Marathon has been rerouted to anticipating herd immunity and being able to return to a world beyond our bubble. Ruth Anne and I took the first step out of our bubble last week to shop at Paper Fiesta wearing masks and using social distancing. We celebrated how Paula Romero-Dunbar was able to keep her dream of her small business alive through the pandemic. I gave her copies of "Hope is a Garden " to sell and told her she could keep the profits. We talked about having the Book Launch Party at the store as we did for "The Adventures of Runnergirl 1953" two years ago.

We have resumed before breakfast runs.

Running in Boston a few weeks before Marathon Weekend often brings magical chance encounters. As we ran around the Reservoir on a glorious Spring morning, we spotted a woman in the distance who we often encountered on our runs. She does meditative walks and T'ai Chi. We had not exchanged more than a few words with a "hi" and comments about the weather.

This morning we spontaneously stopped and shared how wonderful it was to see each other. We asked how each other was and she said, "Well we're still here." "And there are better days ahead," I said.

"Absolutely," she said. "Well you're all vaccinated right?"

We shared with her our vaccine status; Tom gets his 2nd Pfizer shot on Tuesday, Ruth Anne goes for her vaccine on Sunday at Gillette and I go next Wednesday.

"Do you know which one you'll be getting?"

"No," we replied. "How about you?"

 "I've been vaccinated since August. I volunteered for the Moderna study.

"Thank you…wow…" we said to her in unison.

She went on to tell us how she didn't know if she got the placebo or the vaccine but she did get the vaccine. "I had very little side effects. My husband had Pfizer and he had no side effects. Now it's a question of how long it will last but they keep testing me for antibodies and I still have them."

Before we went on our way, I said, "You know we don't even know your name." We introduced ourselves to one another after several years of acknowledging each other with only a nod but little other conversation.

—

8

These kinds of encounters would typically happen on Heartbreak Hill around the time of the Marathon with a focus on the spirit of all that is the Boston Marathon. They are well documented in my Trilogy of Transformation. The focus has shifted from conversations about running and the Boston Marathon to vaccinations and the end of the pandemic. The energy of feeling unified as one returns to Boston as we head toward the finish line of the pandemic.

"Believing is seeing and seeing is Believing!" ~Tom Hanks

On the road to the 2009 Boston Marathon we received many signs in the form of finding money during our training runs. I visualized our success on Marathon Monday and believed with every fiber of my Being that I would successfully cross that finish line.

Last year, while waiting for the results of the election in November, we found an array of change in the street on a run. It gave us hope that it was, in fact, time for a change in Washington and that the tide was going to turn for better days ahead.

The day before we found that change, I wrote this poem included in "Hope is a Garden: Poems and Essays From the 2020 Pandemic":

Believing is Seeing

Worry and fearing thoughts filled with fret
believe what you'll see on positive thoughts be set.
Imagine the outcome feel joy be daring bold
release all the dread a new vision to hold.

Remember the Power Source ignites hope and light
the beautiful story created is well within sight.
Our loving true nature must now prevail
with grit determination and faith through adversity we sail.

A beautiful sunset or a penny that's found
signs of the Presence in abundance surround.
Believing is seeing feel lightness and free
let go and surrender as you abide with Me.

Join together connect with those who feel as you do
whatever the outcome you'll always get through.
A tsunami of hope swells over the land
washing out painful memories like the tide with the sand.

A new day is dawning believe and you'll see
power to create the outcome you wish it to be.
Smile rejoice give thanks let peace now descend
whatever's been rendered is time now to mend!

I remembered the phrase, "or a penny that's found" after we found the change and was able to feel my soul settle during the tumultuous days following the election.

I've been feeling unsettled about my upcoming vaccine appointment this Wednesday. Ruth Anne received her vaccine yesterday and other than a sore arm feels great. We did a lot of meditation and mind/body prep work leading up to her appointment. Tom, our son Autumn, his girlfriend Michelle and many of our friends have received the vaccine and their joy far exceeded any mild side effects they may have experienced. Temporarily stepping back into the medical model to receive a vaccine is an emotional experience.

On this morning's run, I spotted a dime in the middle of the street.

It's dated 2020 and as Tom was quick to point out, 2020 was a year akin to the polio epidemic. What comfort I felt seeing FDR's face on the dime with the word, "Liberty" and on the back, "A torch that stands for liberty, an olive branch that stands for peace, and an oak branch that stands for strength and independence." Receiving the vaccine is a way for us to once again experience our liberty. "E pluribus unum:" out of many, one. Despite all of the divisiveness during the past four years, there is a powerful sense of unity around emerging victorious from the pandemic.

I am always in awe of how I've been touched by grace from an early age and felt a powerful connection to the Divine as I lay paralyzed from the neck down at the tender age of 5 and a half years old. My mother, addicted to prescription pain medication, was more paralyzed than I was and could not care for me. I would have to wait for my father or grandfather to get home to provide basic care. While my mother glared at me smoking a cigarette, I had an out of body experience. That Divine presence stayed with me as I endured unimaginable trauma after contracting paralytic polio.

As I logged onto Twitter I 'just happened' to see a post with a newspaper headline dated April 13, 1955 with the headline, "Salk Polio Vaccine Proves Success; Millions Will Be Immunized Soon." Another column's headline read, "Trial Data Given Efficacy of 80-90% Shown." Ann Arbor Michigan April 12, 1955 – The world learned today that its hope for finding an effective weapon against paralytic polio has been realized.

Believing is seeing; seeing beyond appearances and having faith in positive outcomes. I believed in my ability to heal my life from polio and trauma despite all appearances to the contrary. I believed in my ability to run the Boston Marathon even though I had never run a day in my life. And today, as I briefly revisited my struggle about vax hesitancy, I was reminded by the Divine to have faith and believe seeing a world healed from the COVID-19 pandemic!

"What's considered impossible is just a consensus of outdated beliefs." ~Bernie Siegel, MD

In the mid-1980's, Beth Jordan, a nurse who took care of me during a lengthy hospitalization for a bone infection in my shoulder, told me I needed to heal my life. She introduced me to the work of Dr. Bernie Siegel.

I experienced the truth of his teachings about the power of the mind/body connection through the decades. He talked about how patients under anesthesia can hear the doctor and recommended patients receive positive messages while under anesthesia. I would get very ill after anesthesia until I talked with the anesthesiologist at a pre-op visit about Bernie's teachings. He was all in.

When I came out of anesthesia in the recovery room, I felt a wave of nausea come over me that stopped in the middle and I said, "Can I have a barbeque hamburger please?" The recovery room staff broke out into laughter. They knew the anesthesiologist had given me a suggestion under anesthesia that I would awake feeling comfortable and hungry and craving a barbeque hamburger.

After the diagnosis of Post-Polio Syndrome, I harnessed the power of the mind/body connection to heal my life from the effects of childhood paralytic polio and trauma. I had to feel the healing happening in my body before I saw any outward manifestations of healing.

"When we listen to and draw from our inner wisdom and the great consciousness, we begin the fulfilling and sometimes miraculous journey toward healing." ~Bernie Siegel, MD

As I prepare to receive the vaccine tomorrow, I tune out reported "side effects". My side effects will be joy, hope, celebration, and health and well-being. I recall a poem I wrote shortly after the diagnosis of Post-Polio Syndrome:

Feel the Heal

Feel the heal and heal the fear let goodness Love prevail
holding hands with open heart through adversity we sail.
Living in the present a gift no future and no past
surfing waves of our emotions suffering cannot last.

Feel the heal and heal the fear an illusion that fear is real
let go relax refresh and rest Love and Light can now reveal.
Faith and love no match for fear trust for we can fly
appearances deceiving doubts kiss them all goodbye.

Feel the heal and heal the fear we're held in Loving arms
The Universe magnificent mysterious mystical charms.
We think a door is closing we grasp and hold on tight
miracle's just a breath away release behold its sight.

Feel the heal and heal the fear get out of jail we're free
possibilities are endless in our hands we hold the key.
No longer do we jump through hoops in faith we take a leap
Divine protection safety our life's bounty time to reap.

Feel the heal and heal the fear let our hearts feel calm and peace
worries and anxieties heartache all can cease.
Today's the day we celebrate as we all now feel the heal
courage strength compassion wisdom is all we need to feel.

I recall all the healing I have done harnessing the power of my mind. After a serious left knee injury in December of 2014, I grew new cartilage, dissolved bone spurs, reversed degenerative changes and went on to run 3 consecutive Bermuda Half Marathons despite being

———

14

admonished by the medical community that I should stop running. I was reminded that, as a survivor of paralytic polio, I should have never started running. They said I would need a total knee replacement in a few years based on the findings of the MRI.

As I receive the vaccine tomorrow I will feel the heal and imagine all the wonderful activities we are going to be able to resume in a few weeks. I will tune into the wisdom in all of my cells created by the Divine knowing that, to quote Dr. Joe Dispenza who quoted B.J. Palmer, the founder of chiropractic care, "The Power that made the body, heals the body." I will receive the vaccine with joy and gratitude feeling blessed that we will be able to experience the fullness of life once again.

"You gain strength, courage and confidence by every experience in which you really stop to look fear in the face. You are able to say to yourself, 'I have lived through this horror. I can take the next thing that comes along.' You must do the thing you think you cannot do."
~Eleanor Roosevelt

Last Sunday, Ruth Anne and Tom went to Gillette Stadium where Ruth Anne received her first shot of Moderna. Her brother and his girlfriend, and our friends on social media celebrated with us.

On Tuesday, Tom had his 2nd Pfizer shot at Mass. General Hospital at Assembly Row, and I was on deck for my first shot on Wednesday at Mass. General Hospital/Brigham.

I was blessed to receive two signs that I made the right decision to move ahead with the vaccine when I found a dime on our run and then later that day saw a post on Twitter about the anniversary of when the Salk vaccine was approved in 1955.

As a good runner gets ready for an event, I hydrated and fueled and got myself mentally prepared for the 'event.' I visualized how I wanted things to go from start to finish.

We went on a run to start the day and the weather was glorious!

There was no traffic and we arrived a few minutes before my appointment. We found a parking space with ease after being given masks by the attendant as we entered the parking garage.

We were directed to Station #5 where we were warmly greeted by Emily. As she took my information, I became tearful. 'This is quite emotional for me,' and I explained that I contracted polio in one of the last epidemics in 1959.

She exuded compassion from every fiber of her being. She shared with us that being able to work in the vaccine clinic has been a God

———

send. She is pregnant with twins. We shared our experience as parents of boy/girl twins and I relaxed.

"I believe some people are just sent my way," she said.

As we finished the pre-vaccine interview, she asked me which arm I wanted to use. She came up behind me because she's a lefty.

"You're going to feel so much better after this. Just think about all the things you are going to be able to do once you're fully vaccinated."

What an incredible intention to set as she gave me the vaccine followed up with, "only good energy here."

While we waited for 15 minutes, I cried tears of joy. A feeling of strength and courage surged through me saying, "I did it!"

One of my dear friends from our running club commented on the photo's Facebook post, "Brave girls lead the way."

Emily was an earth angel who gave me a shot in the arm as we all work together to end this pandemic and joyfully move forward in our lives.

I Never Thought....

"Life is not the way it's supposed to be. It's the way it is. The way you cope with it is what makes the difference." ~Virginia Satir

I never thought that I'd have to ponder about whether or not to receive a vaccine for a novel virus after having experienced the polio epidemic as a child. I never thought that I would have to wait 14 months between chiropractic appointments when I went every week to continue to heal the late effects of paralytic polio and trauma. I watched favorite restaurants close and the panic of friends who were small business owners wondering if they would have a business as we began to emerge from the pandemic.

I am in awe of how communities came together to support small business and the strength, resilience and creativity of my friends in business. I never thought I would experience such deep appreciation for in-person shopping at my friend's store Paper Fiesta, the intense anticipation of seeing my chiropractor for an appointment the first week of May and getting my hair cut for the first time in 14 months. Having my daughter give me a trim didn't quite "cut it."

We are emerging from the pandemic. We were so blessed with good health, financial stability and the gift of running in our lives during the pandemic. While I have always lived with an attitude of gratitude, I never thought my gratitude and appreciation could run this deeply in my heart and soul. I appreciate the sights and sounds of Spring in a way I never have before. I feel the joy from posts of people getting together again and grandparents being reunited with grandchildren. It's easy to say that life wasn't supposed to be that way, but the pandemic is the way it was and it's how we live our lives each and every moment of each and every day that counts.

"Adopt the pace of nature: her secret is patience." *~Ralph Waldo Emerson*

We are all eager to experience an end to the pandemic; to travel, to head to the beaches and pools, to go to concerts, Broadway shows, eat at restaurants and for runners to resume racing events. But it's not quite time yet. While vaccinations have helped to flatten the curve, there is still much work to be done in ending the pandemic. While fatigue from this past year is real, this is the time to exercise extraordinary patience to ensure that we can successfully move forward building momentum in ending the public health crisis of the past 14 months.

I look to my garden to adopt the pace of nature.

Last October we bought bulbs and planted them deep in Mother Earth in our yard. I've been taking photos of the progress of our garden watching how, with the ebb and flow of temperatures, the flowers close and halt growth and then resume growth slowly preparing to open the flowers in all of their glory.

It goes at its own pace and we patiently and eagerly anticipate when it will be in full bloom.

We adopted the pace of nature when we did jigsaw puzzles during the pandemic, eagerly awaited news of the next reopening phase, waited for election results, the flattening of the curve of infections and an increase in vaccination rates. Ruth Anne and I have one more vaccine shot aka our "wellness shot" and then have to be patient for two weeks after that before getting together with our friends who are fully vaccinated. We are so close to being able to emerge from the pandemic safely resuming activities that add extra zest to life.

We just need to adopt the pace of Mother Nature. Her secret is patience.

The Magnificence of May   May 2, 2021

"All things seem possible in May." ~Anonymous

As I watched my tulips poke through the once frozen barren ground and bloom, I thought to myself, "What if I had the same hope and faith I had when I planted those bulbs last October trusting they would blossom, and harnessed it in all areas of my life."

So often we want control rather than letting go; to trust in the unseen, to enjoy the mystery and wonder of life, to trust in the most beautiful and positive outcomes and to allow Divine Intelligence to guide. Just as the flowers need to go through the dirt, life can sure get messy at times as we have seen during the harsh winter of the pandemic.

Spring always returns. Last year it was challenging at times to appreciate the glory and splendor of the season. There was a pall that hung over the world as the pandemic claimed lives. We all faced uncertainty and fear trying to get our bearings with a 'new normal.' Initially we were confined to our homes except to go out and exercise. We saw businesses shuttered and restaurants struggled to survive. We had to wear masks everywhere we went and needed to stay socially distant from others. The colors of the season paled as we navigated an unprecedented time in our history.

Yet I always held onto hope and practiced an attitude of gratitude. This year, with vaccines, and signs of hope with metrics shifting to positive trends, May seems even more magnificent than I can remember.

During yesterday's 5K run, we paused to appreciate the bursting colors of Spring and to make note and appreciate nature's splendor. We breathed deeply enjoying the relaxation of the mask mandate for vaccinated persons. Even the swans seem to be embodying the magnificence of May 2021. There is an awakening and emergence from the darkness of the pandemic. On Friday, I had my first visit to a hair salon in 14 months. What a treat to have long unruly locks transform into a beautiful new style for Spring.

Yesterday was seedling pick up day at Ruth Anne's ReVision Urban Farm. After our run and before we headed to the Farm, we ordered take out from Brothers and Sisters Cafe in Brookline Village. For the first time in 14 months we ate outside at a picnic bench among other people (socially distant with masks up when we weren't eating). There was a street festival and the energy was electric!

The last time Ruth Anne volunteered at the Farm was in January when the Farm Manager and Senior Grower were plodding through the cold, harsh winter. We returned to a vibrant, bustling community of staff and volunteers lovingly distributing the seedlings for customers to have their own gardens!

This week I receive my second "wellness shot" and get to see my chiropractor after 14 months of no treatments! There is a spiritual awakening of so many emotions experiencing "firsts" after so many months of adapting to "nots." My heart overflows with gratitude and relief, anticipatory joy for reunions and experiences we once took for granted.

It's already a magnificent May as the earth and its Beings awaken to hope, possibilities and a return to activities that bring so much joy to life.

"I am convinced that unconditional love is the most powerful known stimulant of the immune system. If I told patients to raise their blood levels of immune globulins or killer T cells, no one would know how. But if I can teach them to love themselves and others fully, the same changes happen automatically. The truth is: love heals." ~Bernie Siegel, MD

Three weeks from today marks the 14th anniversary of when I left my award-winning career as a VA social worker to heal my life from the once devastating effects of childhood paralytic polio and severe child abuse at the hands of family members. As I was reflecting on this anniversary and social media's Tuesday transformation theme, I reflected on how the first step in my healing journey was to learn how to love myself.

Enduring years of abuse at the hands of family members and taunting from peers because I was different from them, lugging an ankle to hip leg brace, walking with a limp and not being able to contribute to my team's efforts in gym class, took quite a toll on mind, body and soul. I had been familiar with Bernie Siegel's work since the 1980's. Although I had not read "Love, Medicine and Miracles" in many years, the story of Evy McDonald and her miraculous recovery from ALS stayed with me. She was also a polio survivor and after the diagnosis of ALS, decided she was not going to die hating her body. She literally loved herself well.

After my diagnosis, I reached out to Bernie as I had done through the years for guidance and what he calls being a "rebirthing coach" as my "Chosen Dad" to re-parent me and teach me how to re-parent myself. I joined his Forum, revisited his books and explored the works of other mind/body luminaries. The gift of poetry was ignited in my soul after getting still and asking for Divine Guidance. Themes of gratitude, forgiveness, and self-love helped to heal my past. Imagination and visualization for a future very different than the one the doctors predicted for me of preparing to spend the rest of my life in a wheelchair inspired me to heal mind, body and soul.

—

I was a workaholic consumed with the needs of my patients, their families, my Team and my family. I didn't know how to practice self-care and forgot to how to enjoy life. I had to learn how to live again and running provided me with just the path I needed to rediscover life. Running was a great metaphor for the fullness of life and discovering my strength, resilience, beauty, grace, courage and being surrounded by love from the running community for my journey on the road to the 2009 Boston Marathon.

Fourteen years ago I faced an uncertain future after a devastating diagnosis but I transformed the experience to learn how to love and how to live. I carry Bernie's message with me as I prepare to receive my second vaccine.

"One's attitude towards oneself is the single most important factor in healing and staying well." ~Bernie Siegel, MD

Prior to the diagnosis of Post-Polio Syndrome in December of 2006, I had an estranged relationship with my body. I had to dissociate in order to survive years of abuse at the hands of family members. While harnessing my intellectual prowess enabled me to have a successful career as a VA social worker, all those years of ignoring my body's needs took a toll. The diagnosis was a blessing and a wake-up call as I reconnected with the precious treasure of my body that is the temple for my soul.

I immersed in the teachings of mind/body luminaries and was able to heal my life from the effects of paralytic polio and trauma.

After conquering my fear, I received the first shot in my arm.

Other than a sore arm, I had no side effects. My son and his girlfriend had a much easier time of it after their 2nd shot but my husband experienced side effects of fatigue, dizziness and irregular heartbeat and breathing. His doctor reassured him that those are within the range of 'normal' side effects but it gave me pause about getting my 2nd shot. I had also seen a lot of Facebook posts about friends experiencing side effects after their 2nd shot. Yet there was no turning back.

I know the power of the mind/body connection and treated preparing for my 2nd "wellness shot" like I was training for race day. Hydration, pre-'race' fueling, meditation, visualization and letting my body know the outcome I expected were the order of the day.

On Monday, I attended David Hamilton's monthly meeting of The Personal Development Club. We discuss topics related to mind/body connection, kindness, mindfulness and therapies outside of traditional medicine. David's presentation focused on the use of crystals. He inspired me to take a crystal with me and hold it in my left hand while I received the vaccine.

Yesterday we went for a morning run despite the cool rainy weather. I made sure to enjoy the sensuous sights, sounds and smells of Springtime to take with me into the sterile Brigham/Mass General building where I would receive my vaccine.

I had a turkey sandwich with spinach on dark bread with a lot of sparkling water. For dessert I had a banana and a FlavaNatural Chocolate bar that's known to reduce inflammation.

I could feel the nerves kick in. On the drive in town, I took deep breaths and used visualization while tightly holding my crystal.

We found a parking space right away but got lost on our way to the clinic after leaving the parking garage. We arrived right on time. I asked if Emily was working (the nurse I had for shot #1) but she had just taken a lunch break. Ruth Anne accompanied me this time and they asked if she wanted to get a vaccine. Those frenetic days of trying to get an appointment are behind us. Ruth Anne gets her second "wellness shot" on Sunday at Gillette Stadium.

I had a lovely nurse who went over everything with me about the possibility of side effects after the 2nd shot that one might not have experienced after the first one. "I have my crystal right here. I've been meditating and hydrating so I'll be fine." "Yes you will," she agreed. "And it's a very quick shot."

While waiting for the required 15 minutes post-vaccine I took deep breaths despite wearing two masks. I could feel the anxiety around getting the vaccines begin to yield to a sense of relief and joy.

We texted my son who was overjoyed that we are close to all being fully vaccinated.

I continued to hydrate all day today and other than a little arm soreness felt fine. "Well I did it!" I thought to myself as the day drew to a close.

———

25

When We Find Ourselves in a Strange New World   May 10, 2021

"The wings of transformation are born of patience and struggle."
~Janet S. Dickens

We are emerging from the cocoon of our "bubbles" and the insular world we inhabited during these past 14 months. We are on a journey of transformation as we find our wings and freedom in this strange new world where science guides us about the risks of different behaviors based on the trends of the COVID-19 virus.

"After approximately 10 to 14 days as a chrysalis, the butterfly is ready to emerge. When the butterfly emerges from its chrysalis, its wings are small and wet, and the butterfly cannot yet fly. The butterfly must pump fluids from its abdomen through the veins in its wings, which causes the wings to expand to their full size. Next, the wings must dry and the butterfly must exercise flight muscles before it can fly." ~from Butterfly School

The time of transition from lockdown to quarantine to easing of restrictions albeit with a lot of precautions and fear still running rampant, to this time of decreased infections, deaths and hospitalizations with increased vaccination rates feels like the butterfly's wet wing phase of transformation.

Yesterday we 'celebrated' Mother's Day by going to Gillette Stadium for Ruth Anne to receive her 2nd vaccine.

In years past we would go to Cape Cod for a day trip and eat out at one of our favorite Falmouth restaurants. We took a selfie to document we are all vaccinated wearing double masks, and included the giant screen at Gillette that indicated the number of vaccines administered to date.

We ate outdoors at a restaurant for the first time in 14 months! There were strange new rituals such as no menus but a code to put in the phone to access the menu. Our waiter and all the staff wore masks, and patrons wore masks except while eating or drinking. Silverware was wrapped in a linen napkin and the waiter was careful to keep them wrapped as he placed them on the table. There were no salt and pepper shakers or ketchup bottles. A small plastic container of ketchup with a lid was served with our meal. Since it was our first time dining out at a restaurant in 14 months, Tom took a photo to document the occasion.

The CBS Sporting Club restaurant, previously known as CBS Scene was our go to place before the annual July 4th celebration Finish at the 50 race. We were struck by how strangely quiet it was for a beautiful Spring Mother's Day in May. The usual excitement and hype for summer concerts, upcoming New England Revolution games and the Finish at the 50 race were strangely absent. The steady stream of cars were headed to the East and West vaccination clinics.

During this morning's meditation, I reflected on the strange new world I encountered after June 5, 1959, the day I contracted paralytic polio. One of the many many silver linings of this pandemic is that I have been able to more deeply heal the wounds from having contracted paralytic polio despite having had 5 vaccines. It seems that there is such a thing as "breakthrough cases" of COVID-19 in people who have been vaccinated though it is extremely rare. That might be an explanation for how I contracted polio as I was playing with my best friend whose mom was not vaccinated. We contracted it on the same day. As I lay paralyzed on the couch time stood still for me. My friends finished kindergarten year and had a graduation ceremony. When I returned to 1st grade, I returned to a strange new world wearing an ankle to hip leg brace and using crutches for mobility. My beautiful long hair was cut into a pixie cut because my mother and grandmother felt it was too much for them to have to take care of my long hair on top of the other demands for providing care for me. I was a stranger to myself from the lithe active ballerina I was before I dropped to the ground in gym class with absolutely no warning!

I honed my intellectual prowess and graduated as high school valedictorian. After receiving my MSW from Boston College, I had an award-winning social work career at the VA until my world came to a screeching halt after the diagnosis of Post-Polio Syndrome in December of 2006. I entered a strange new world of rehabilitation and prognostication of what life would look like for me as I aged. I got still and asked for Divine Guidance. What an incredible journey of transformation I experienced.

It can be overwhelming and frightening when we find ourselves in a strange new world. We are making the transition from wearing face masks whenever we were out in public to being able to do outdoor activities mask-free. We are making plans for the first time in 14 months. Tom and Ruth Anne gave me tickets to "Jagged Little Pill" for the October 24th matinee for my Mother's Day present. We decided to drive to New York rather than take the train despite being fully vaccinated so we can enjoy the ride without masks. We will need to present proof of vaccination and I imagine that New York City will have a different post-pandemic vibe.

There is discomfort in experiencing the strangeness of our times. But it is also an extraordinary opportunity for growth and transformation and to experience a deeper and richer appreciation for life.

We find ourselves in a strange new world awakened to the preciousness and fragility of life, our vulnerability, the need for social change and justice, and to change our habits if we are going to preserve our precious Mother Earth. We find ourselves in a strange new world filled with hope, resilience, infinite possibilities and opportunities for creation and innovation.

Keep the Faith

When challenges arise
keep the faith
close to your open heart
be grateful.
See blessings
on horizon wonderful happenings
waiting for you.

See signs
as angels guide
guardians of your Well-Being
always by your side
believing is seeing
joy in journeying
navigating turbulent waters
powerful oars to negotiate rapids
deliciousness in Oneness
strength of Source deep within.

Feel the rush
ride the waves
heart pounding
keep the faith
safely arriving on shore.

Here's to embracing the strangeness of our times and finding
ourselves uplifted and inspired when we come out on the other side.

"Gratitude is the best medicine. It heals your mind, your body and your spirit. And attracts more things to be grateful for."
~Anonymous

Do you have little post-pandemic things that you are grateful for and make you smile?

Here are a few of mine:
Bananas and potatoes that were in short supply
My favorite floss threaders from CVS that had been out of stock for weeks
Toilet paper - duh
Grated carrots from Trader Joe's
Our favorite brand of orange juice at Star Market
Finding puzzle pieces that fit

What a difference a year makes!

I am deeply grateful and blessed that we can now run without masks although we do have one with us at all times.

This Spring seems to be more magnificent than any Spring I can remember. The morning sun's reflection on the Reservoir reflected the joy and gratitude we feel in our hearts. Our immediate family have all received 2 doses of vaccine. My son and his girlfriend are going to be eating outside at a restaurant for the first time in 14 months. For the first time in 14 months we have plans on the calendar. Businesses are easing screening restrictions but remain in compliance with safety guidelines from the CDC. I look forward to when we will no longer need to have our temperatures taken or fill out health surveys before appointments at the dentist, chiropractor or hair salon and am so grateful we once again have access to these services. During lockdown, we had no idea when we would be able to access them again. Fourteen months later there is so much to be grateful for. I am grateful for how deeply appreciation runs in my heart and soul.

"Challenge is a dragon with a gift in its mouth. Tame the dragon and the gift is yours." ~Noela Evans

I've known challenges from an early age. At 5 years old I contracted paralytic polio in one of the last epidemics in the United States. Seeing what is happening with COVID-19, I now believe I was one of the 'breakthrough' cases since I had received 5 vaccines and there was no indication mine was one of the 'bad batches' that happened from a lack of quality control in 1959. I endured years of abuse at the hands of family members from the age of 8 until my father ended his life at the age of 17. Those challenges turned out to be the greatest gifts in my life informing the woman I am today. At the age of 53, the gift of polio kept on giving as I was diagnosed with Post-Polio Syndrome, a progressive neuromuscular disease by Western Medicine Standards. I experienced a joyous albeit challenging journey of transformation after the diagnosis.

The lessons learned and wisdom garnered throughout those challenges held me in good stead during the COVID-19 pandemic. We looked beyond fear and grief to find the silver linings; the treasures of the experience that will stay with us moving forward in our lives.

Since gyms were closed, we couldn't swim or use cardio equipment. We went outside for runs and walks. There was only one day that the weather prevented us from getting outside. We knew how vital it was to exercise and get plenty of fresh air and sunshine regardless of the weather. Running or walking 3-4 times/week with extra mini walks in between around the neighborhood built strength. Rather than breathing in air with the smell of chlorine, we breathed in fresh air and took into our hearts and souls the change of the seasons.

Tom worked from home and not having a commute, albeit a short one, gave us time to be together, prepare wonderful meals or do take out enjoying leisurely meals together. Breakfast was unhurried and we were able to do early morning or noon time runs together.

Our meditation practice strengthened in depth and frequency. Because I was unable to have chiropractic treatments, I once again tapped into my body's tremendous capacity to heal with an ever deepening connection to Source.

We have a deep appreciation for our home and our yard. For the first time, we planted a flower garden. Every time I looked at that little plot of ground, it was a reminder of hope and faith. What excitement I felt as the little sprouts poked through the once frozen earth and then bloomed into magnificent tulips. We planted our tomato seedlings and marigolds in the raised bed we built last year. We had an incredible harvest last year that we shared with neighbors with masks and social distancing. We developed a greater sense of community in our neighborhood sharing in the somber mood of last year to find ways to uplift each other while keeping apart. This year that connection remains and is transformed into joy and hugs.

We were all challenged to allow our true selves to shine through beyond clothes, makeup and hair styles. We were called upon to use humor and ingenuity when it came to our hair. We had many wonderful belly laughs as we attempted to style each other's hair. What an incredible treat to go to the salon after 14 months; an experience I will never again take for granted!

If it weren't for the pandemic, I am not sure how motivated we all would have been to get out the vote as we did. Whatever your politics may be, the truth is our democracy was threatened and incompetence at the highest levels of government were exposed by the pandemic. The power of the vote and 'we the people' was a silver lining that shined through the shroud of darkness hovering over our nation.

As time goes on, I am sure other silver linings of the pandemic will become apparent to me and to us as a global community.

These past 14 months have tested our mettle while offering gifts and treasures that will forever be a part of the tapestry of our lives.

Opening Daze

The day we'd all been waiting for
time to open be together be free
after living under a cloud of fear
we're feeling profound hesitancy.

Most people have been fully vaxed
a phrase once foreign now eerily commonplace
like a swimmer wading into ocean's cold
we tentatively move into each other's space.

So many questions and fear arise
is the pandemic now at its end
or is this perhaps only a lull
with another outbreak round the bend.

And while we're trusting science
metrics statistics the order of the day
I set my sights on trusting Source
transforming fear let Love light the way.

A year and some months later
once masked we smiled only with our eyes
we now unveil our transformations
soul lessons learned we are now more wise.

Emerging from our fog and haze
may we bathe in love from each other's heart
entering into this new normal world
as a new life chapter we start.

"There is a light within all of us that is home and safe. It is very powerful. Where nothing can harm you, no matter the storm."
~Anonymous

"Running in the rain makes me feel that I can handle the whole world." ~Anonymous

Waking up to the sound of pouring rain on a day when we're scheduled to run always begs the question, "Should we swap a strength training day for our run day?" The forecast called for rain all weekend. I knew in the depths of my heart and soul that we needed to get out for our run today. I got still as we put on our guided meditation to start the day.

During breakfast, we read the articles about Governor Baker's proclamation that all COVID-19 restrictions were lifted as of midnight on 5/28. We shared the excitement about the end of the pandemic and how blessed we have been and are to experience good health while also acknowledging a tinge of fear wondering, "Is this too soon?"

We couldn't dwell there because the almost record setting cold day for Memorial Day Weekend was beckoning us to get our run on. We debated about where we should run and opted for a run around the neighborhood and the small Reservoir on Route 9 knowing we could stop at the house if we needed a change of clothes. We reminded ourselves of when we used to train in weather conditions worse than this as we trained for the 2009 Boston Marathon for our long runs.

"It's where we put our attention and mindset," I reminded Team McManus. It was hard to believe that two days ago we were in tank tops needing fans to cool off the house and today we needed winter running pants, jackets, hats and gloves. That's weather in New England for you.

We allowed joy to flow through us opening our arms (and hearts) wide singing and splashing in the puddles.

During my morning meditation, a poem started to flow through me that I finished after our run.

Morning Rain

Tear shaped raindrops on window pane
as we are preparing to live life again
an outpouring of emotions-sadness, grief, relief dawn of new day
joining hearts and hands together tentatively finding our way.

Spirits once dampened by dreaded disease
take stock and take pause as routines we unfreeze
though the day's skies are cloudy a light burns so bright
casting away fourteen months filled with flooding of fright.

In the stillness of morning as rain poured from the sky
I was tempted to wonder to ponder ask why
but I know it's a mystery so I reigned in that thought
taking deep breaths chest no longer drawn taut.

As gratitude bubbled up from the depth of my heart
with a smile on my lips as new day time to start
heading out on a run filled with laughter and play
no masks on our faces heavy burdens no longer weigh.

Soaked to the skin splashed in puddles galore
mud stained and chilled contentment needing nothing more
radiating Love from Source our troubles are light
healing on horizon is now well within sight.

We felt cleansed, refreshed and renewed after our run in the rain
changing into warm comfy clothes to enjoy the rest of the first day
of lifted COVID-19 restrictions.

"Let your smile change the world; never let the world change your smile." ~Anonymous

On Saturday's run, we heard a passing runner yell out, "No masks!" I had to ask Tom and Ruth Anne, 'What did he say?' because, for the past 15 months, there have been on occasion, grumblings and snarky comments whether we wore a mask or had momentarily taken our masks off on a run.

They confirmed he said "no masks" and all three of us smiled. We realized for the first time in 15 months that we did not need to wear a mask or have one handy while out on a run. How glorious to be able to smile at one another.

One of the most challenging parts of the pandemic for me was needing to wear a mask.

On what would have been Marathon Monday in April 2020, we didn't have masks yet and used scarves over our mouths during a 2.62 mile run. One of my friends saw our Facebook post and said, "Do you need masks?" I told her that the public health commissioner of Brookline sent out a mandate that all residents of Brookline have to wear a mask in public. "No do you need masks. I am making them." In exchange for her sending us masks, we made a donation to her favorite charity.

It was an intense struggle for me to have to wear a mask. As a trauma survivor, it was intensely uncomfortable to have my mouth and nose covered, yet I knew it had to be done for the highest good. I struggled with whether or not to get vaccinated. What a surprise to have the mask mandate lifted for those of us who are fully vaccinated.

People always tell my daughter and me that we have beautiful smiles that light up a room. It was challenging to not allow these past 15 months to change that smile.

On May 13th, President Biden said,: *"If you're fully vaccinated and can take your mask off, you have earned the right to do something that Americans are known for all around the world: greeting others with a smile. With a smile. So, it is a good day for the country."*

It feels miraculous to be able to see people smile again. Smiles seem to be more radiant filled with joy and relief than before March 13, 2020.

"A smile is contagious, let's start an epidemic." *~Anonymous*

Maskless

Take off the mask
shedding fears
allow tears to flow
we made it through.

Fourteen months of angst
now ending
grateful to be alive
eager to hug
joy and laughter
Spirits shining through.

Resilience reflected
sparkling eyes
lives transformed
lines of age and wisdom revealed.

Bask in the light
warmth beaming from radiant smiles
happy to be
at last
maskless.

"The best times in life are usually random, unplanned and completely spontaneous." ~Anonymous

We had started and stopped heading to Cape Cod as things began to open up and we were fully vaccinated. Before Memorial Day Weekend and Governor Baker's lifting of the restrictions for COVID-19, we gave pause to heading to the Cape. Where could we go to the bathroom? How long of a wait would there be to get a table at a restaurant? Could we enjoy our time still needing to wear a mask in certain situations?

When we woke up Monday morning, it was an uncharacteristically cool Memorial Day. There was drizzle and fog with the forecast calling for rain/drizzle/fog in Boston and in Falmouth. After meditation, we spontaneously decided it was the perfect day to head to our happy place where we had not been since February of 2020.

I suggested that we do our run in Brookline and then head to the Cape but Ruth Anne suggested we do our run along Falmouth Heights Beach. We trusted that we would have access to a bathroom when we needed it. Since capacity restrictions were lifted, we'd be able to find a good place to eat.

I felt the excitement as we pulled out of the driveway to go the farthest distance away from Brookline in 15 months.

I was overcome with emotion seeing road signs we hadn't seen for what seemed like forever.

We knew that the beautiful Cape Cod Canal was below us just beyond the dense fog as we crossed over the Bourne Bridge.

Our first stop was Falmouth Heights Beach. My breath caught to see it again. Only shadows of letters remained on the sign for the British Beer Company where we would have a pit stop while on a run at the beach, order a sparkling water at the bar and return for English pub style food later in the day. It always reminded us of pubs in Bermuda. Fortunately the new staff were kind enough to let us use the facilities when we needed to as we explained how the British Beer Company always let us use their bathroom. I felt a lump in my throat to see how the place was changed from where we would often go during trips to Falmouth especially during the Falmouth Road Race weekend.

We had a slow place for our 5K enjoying the scenery along the way reminiscing about the times we visited Falmouth when the kids were young. While our clothes were damp, our spirits were high from breathing in the salty sea air and being in our happy place once more.

The next big question of the day was where to have lunch. We decided on The Flying Bridge but it was a very different Flying Bridge from the last time we were there in the Fall of 2019. The outdoor area where they were serving was encased with plastic all the way around. There were lamps for warmth but it was uncomfortably warm and claustrophobic. We opted to head to Main Street to another one of our favorite restaurants, Anejo Mexican Bistro. The wait staff eagerly dried off the chairs at the outdoor table and greeted us with warm smiles. There was a long line to get in for indoor dining but no wait for an outdoor table where we dined on delicious burritos and tacos.

After lunch, we supported local business at Eight Cousins Bookstore and savored every moment on Main Street. Eight Cousins Bookstore had a sign on the door requesting customers wear masks since not all staff were fully vaccinated. We smiled with our eyes letting staff know we were happy to comply with their request. We had our traditional ice cream from Ben and Bill's Ice Cream Emporium before heading home. With hearts (and bellies) full we drove home excited for a summer that President Joe Biden said we all deserve after a very long dark winter.

Spontaneity was not a word in our vocabulary during the pandemic. We had to plan runs, trips to the grocery store, make sure we had masks and could maintain social distancing. There were no trips to the beach during the height of summer or trips to the Cape. What a joy to allow the day to unfold unplanned, unplugged and for the most part, maskless and spontaneous!

Gratitude and Grace

A joyous jubilation
a jamboree
freedom
and yet...
a heaviness in heart
empty store fronts
empty seats at dinner tables

How do we heal from the carnage?

Gratitude heals the hole
making us whole
grace reigns from clouds of despair
sifting and sorting through rubble
treasures found.

Strength and resilience
beyond what we ever believed
was possible.

"The beautiful moon is an antidepressant. Love for her light is in every heart because she is so friendly, loving and forgiving."
~Debasish Mridha, MD

The Gift of the Golden Moon

Heart pounding
my 4am wake-up call
residue of fright fifteen months later

Birds' songs serenade me
a lullaby to quell my quickened heart rate

Angels' precious presence speak in whispers
"Look up!"
My breath caught breathing in cool fresh air
eyes behold a waning crescent moon
golden illumination
transition from night to dawn.

"All is well" I repeated
image emblazoned on closed eyelids
Divine Love beams
powerful laser to cut ties to fear
bathing my body in Truth.

Quiet busy mind forlorn and fretting
worries warrant prayer
in stillness illumination ignites my spark of faith
emboldened after beholding golden moon
lulled to sleep by trust
I drift
refreshed
I awaken to the dawn of a new day.

In the wake of the pandemic, I continue to experience trauma dreams. They are not as frequent or intense as they were during the height of the pandemic, but continue to be present. During the height of the pandemic, it was a challenge to get back to sleep after a trauma dream but last night's dream brought with it a beautiful gift. I had never thought to get out of bed and look out the window after a trauma dream. I had never seen the moon at 4 in the morning. It was a Divine experience. Throughout the pandemic, I experienced a stronger connection to Source with more frequent meditations, being a vessel for poetry that strengthened my faith and asking my angels for strength and guidance during challenging moments.

Although I awakened at 4am and was up for about an hour, I woke up refreshed and ready to go on a run at 7am. While we wore our winter running clothes last Saturday, we wore tank tops and tees with shorts. We took our frozen water bottles out of the freezer while we ate breakfast and debated about where we wanted to run. Since all restrictions are lifted, we knew that traffic would be heavy and any place near water would have large crowds.

We chose to savor the beauty of our Reservoir and the luxury of smiling at runners passing by and at people sitting on benches enjoying our new found freedom as we emerge from the pandemic. It was one of my best runs in a while with negative splits and pouring sweat. I love how sweat continues to pour after the run is over.

Ruth Anne went on to run another 5K while Tom and I spent quality time together. We debriefed about the stress of the past week and how excited we are to move beyond both the pandemic and Ruth Anne's health challenges. We had a leisurely picnic lunch in our yard followed by much needed yard work but not before we put on our bathing suits, fired up our sprinkler and remembered what it's like to feel like a carefree child in summer time.

"If you watch how nature deals with adversity, continually renewing itself, you can't help but learn." ~Bernie Siegel, MD

The tree in our neighbor's yard has not bloomed in several years. We often said that the tree was lonely for its original owners who passed away and their children sold the property. The property is now being used as a rental property. The new tenants are lovely and wanted to know how to help the tree bloom. We suggested that they lovingly trim the dead branches, water the soil and see what happens.

And what beauty happened with vivid purple flowers.

This post-pandemic season is an extraordinary time for renewal. Purple, reds, pink, and even yellow flowers seem to be showing eye-popping color. Of course perception is a big part of seeing but many of my friends in social media are making the same comments about how magnificent Spring in Boston is this year.

There's also extraordinary renewal of joy, grateful hearts, hope and celebrations.

We have been pruned during the pandemic needing to socially distance, change our habits, forego traditional celebrations and gatherings finding ourselves in a very strange new world.

Since Governor Baker lifted all restrictions, there has been a blossoming of gratitude and photos of graduates with their families beaming with an indescribable joy celebrating the milestone of graduation in the context of a pandemic. What would mark an ordinary milestone in the lives of graduates from kindergarten through college has been transformed into an extraordinarily emotional experience. We celebrate as a community deeply blessed and grateful that ceremonies and celebrations can happen once more.

Prior to resuming pre-pandemic activities, there was a collective sense of fatigue and weariness. While most adapted to wearing

—

masks, we were tired of having to don masks wherever we went.

"Will this ever be over?" was the question of the day. We owe it to ourselves to take the time we need to make this transition from living under the cloud of the pandemic to this time of extraordinary renewal.

I am so excited for what takes root and blossoms as we grow in love, faith, hope, joy, hugs, gratitude, realizing our resilience and strength to navigate life's adversity taking our cue from how nature renews itself.

Renewal

Weariness and wariness
when will this pandemic ever end?
Asking how and where and why
on my faith I must depend.
Yet being only human
I'm tired to the bone
also knowing that it's pointless
to whine, complain and moan.

It's been the longest darkest winter
holding tight to the end of my rope
digging deep to do soul work
clinging closely feeling hope.
As winter's ground began to thaw
buds of renewal came into view
sensing finish line's in sight
tough miles but we made through.

Fully vaccinated
a new phrase with thumbs up pic
once deadly corona virus
our antibodies now can flick.

And with the grace of Springtime
brilliant colors burst on the scene
hearts opened with blossoming flowers
purples, pinks, yellows and reds - grass of vibrant green.

Celebrations fill social media
a kind of joy extraordinaire
caps and gowns donned with relief and pride
so much emotion fills the air.
A scene so very different
than 15 months ago
patiently (or not) waiting for these moments
giving life that special glow.

Emerging from winter's darkness
now time to live life with delight
leaving behind the pain of the past
snuffing out those moments of fright.
Let us gather the lessons
moving forward to light our way
and appreciate every moment
of each and every day.

"The best and most beautiful things in the world cannot be seen or even touched. They must be felt with the heart." ~Helen Keller

As I scroll through my social media newsfeed and receive emails about upcoming in person events, I find myself overcome with emotion. Tears overflow from a grateful heart that life can resume with in person celebrations and that the lights will be back on Broadway. My like-hearted friends have been sharing videos that mark the end of the pandemic and the start of moving forward in our lives.

As tears overflow, goosebumps appear on my arms and I feel tingles all over. I allow the tears of joy and goosebumps to wash away the fears of the past 15 months and make space for wonderful new adventures.

In August, my son and his girlfriend are coming to visit. The twins haven't seen each other in person in 4 years. We were hoping to go last summer for their 33rd birthday but the pandemic quickly squashed those plans. There is a sense of urgency to seizing the moment and savoring life to the fullest.

In October we are going to New York City to see "Jagged Little Pill". We have not been to New York in years and are so excited to return. As one Broadway actor recently said, "Intermission is over!" I feel tears well up and goosebumps all over as we anticipate these two trips.

With every post about graduations, birthdays, reunions with grandparents and lights turning back on in stadiums, businesses and theaters, I feel the rush of emotion that is felt deep in my heart in the wake of these past 15 months.

Our air purifiers are put away. There's more space on the top shelf of the bookshelf by the door that once had an overflow of masks that needed to be worn everywhere, and laundered on a regular basis. Every day there's always something that triggers joyful tears and goosebumps as we heal together and emerge from the pandemic into the glorious light of late Spring.

Space

A few masks for just in case
a welcome empty space on bookshelf by the door
air purifiers stored in basement
floored we need them no more
untie stomach's knot
space to freely breathe
freedom from havoc pandemic wrought

Savoring summertime's sacred moments
maskless
leisurely neighborhood after dinner stroll
basking in spectacular sunsets

Once seeing life through pandemic's lens
gratitude floods heart and soul
senses delighted by simple pleasures
time to breathe
space to be
and live life anew.

Contentment

When turmoil of world roils
thoughts boiling over
confinement
why
whining
wishing
wanting
waiting

STOP

gratitude unlocks door
opens heart
deep breath
transforms complaining

Look around
notes to self
simple pleasures
kitty cuddles
quiet evening at home
sumptuous summer fruit
sweet fragrance after the rain
reunion hugs
taste of first snowflakes
icicles like diamonds on trees
splendor of autumn leaves.

Piece by piece
weaving together
tapestry from the Divine
peace and contentment.

"I can't go back to yesterday-because I was a different person then."
~Lewis Carroll

"I hope everything can get back to normal" is a common post by friends in social media now that metrics and statistics indicate that the pandemic is coming to an end in the United States. And what a human sentiment to experience, but can we ever go back to before?

During last night's before bed meditation, I had muscle memory from when I was a beautiful ballerina before I contracted paralytic polio at the tender age of 5 and a half years old. The phrase, 'Back to before, everything is different' came to me along with the realization that I could never go back to my life before I contracted paralytic polio and endured years of trauma at the hands of family members. I lost my sense of innocence and not being able to have that sense of unbridled joy that children should get to experience, but gained spiritual wisdom far beyond my years. I developed a strength of character and discipline that held me in good stead navigating my young adult and adult life.

"Out of suffering have emerged the strongest souls; the most massive characters are seared with scars." ~Kahil Gibran

As Tony Robbins once said, *"It's never too late to have a happy childhood."*

Fast forward to today as photos of graduations, weddings, events, road racing, reunions, gatherings, flinging masks in the air at bars, as the mask mandate was lifted and a touting of returning to life as it was before, but there is no more back to before. We live in a world changed by a virus that swept through, and in many countries still sweeping through, wreaking havoc with every aspect of life.

This afternoon, the Heath School 8th grade graduation took place in the "Little Field" across from our house. Our twins graduated in 2002. As much as we wanted to go back to before 9/11, everything was different. My daughter and I reflected on how their lives were changed that day. I had to stay in place as a social worker at the VA and the school personnel had to support the children who heard the news about airplanes hitting the World Trade Center.

The families, graduates and school personnel for the class of 2021 had to endure a year unlike any other. As families and graduates arrived for the celebration, we could feel how different this year is from any other year. There is usually a stage where the students sit and there are rows of seats for the families. This year, there was a circle with a stage in the middle where students received their diplomas. Students and families were dressed to the nines which is highly unusual for the 8th grade graduation at Heath.

Ruth Anne and I had a full on ugly cry hearing the music, seeing staff and students' procession and the cheers as students walked to receive their hard earned diplomas.

We clapped as the Principal had staff, then families and graduates stand making remarks about resilience, strength and community. He noted how the students brought light and joy in the midst of very dark times. After the ceremony, we said hello to one of Ruth Anne's former teachers whose son graduated 8th grade and congratulated them both.

We spoke with the Principal letting him know how moved we were. He said, "It was quite a year and on a day like today, it all seems like a blur."

As much as we'd love to go back to before traumatic events occur, it's just not possible. As Lewis Carroll said, we are not the same people we were yesterday. The question then becomes, how do we emerge into the light having gone through darkness and turmoil, and bring forward light and joy.

Back to Before

Yearning to go back to before
when tragedy struck
rewind the tape
Ah if only it were that easy
life in rear view mirror
an illusion
of easy times
romanticized
idealized.

What about now?

Gratitude and appreciation
flow deeply in veins
once vain
priorities change.

Celebrate triumph
resilience and strength
golden nuggets
treasure found
Phoenix rising
after surrender
yielding to what was
right of way
rites of passage
to forge a path
faith the torch that lights the way
everything is different
infinite possibilities
on our new landscape of life.

Father's Day Reflections 2021

"Family isn't always blood. It's the people in your life who want you in theirs; the ones who accept you for who you are. The ones who would do anything to see you smile and who love you no matter what." ~Anonymous

Father's Day celebrations had always been difficult for me. My social media newsfeed filled with pictures of adoring posts about how wonderful their fathers were or are. I realize there are many out there who had circumstances similar to mine and may have experienced the same pangs as I did. Yet this year, in the wake of the pandemic, that ache is transformed and transcended. I feel deep abiding joy for those who share in the love of fathers and grandfathers and who can once again be reunited for Father's Day Celebrations. My heart overflows with compassion for those whose beloved fathers have died and people feel moved to share their photos from years past. And my heart overflows with gratitude as I reflect on those who have been like a father to me.

Joe Stetz was my swimming counselor when I attended Badger Day Camp. When I was 10 years old, after two failed camp experiences, my physiatrist who was helping me recover from polio, suggested I go to Badger Day Camp because they focused on swimming and opened their hearts to all abilities. Joe was on track to become a competitor in the 1964 Olympics in the Butterfly but instead he chose to become a physician.

There were only two other campers competing in the end of Camp Olympics in the butterfly and Joe, with his soulful brown eyes told me that I needed to be the third competitor. I was guaranteed a place on the medal stand. I couldn't believe that he wanted me to compete. I told him all of my fears while not revealing what was happening in my home life but focusing on the effects of paralytic polio. He told me he would work with me one on one to conquer my fears. He nurtured within me the heart of a champion. I finished my race long after the other swimmers touched the wall. It didn't matter to Joe.

He lovingly extended a hand to me to help me out of the pool. He walked with me to the medal stand where I received a bronze plaque for 3rd place. He believed in me as a father would and nourished my abilities. I drew from what he taught me after the diagnosis of Post-Polio Syndrome when I decided to run the 2009 Boston Marathon despite all the odds. His last day of camp hug left a lasting imprint on my heart and soul. There were many times during the pandemic when I drew on its strength.

I discovered his Death Notice in the Boston Globe in December of 2004 and did a google search to learn more about the incredible life of the man who helped me navigate the turbulent waters of my childhood. I was stunned to discover that we worked at St. Elizabeth's Medical Center at the same time when I worked as a social worker on the inpatient geriatric psychiatric unit.

I 'just happened' to be standing next to a woman at the starting line of the 2017 Bermuda 10K waiting for Tom to begin his race. As runners often do, we struck up a conversation. She was a nurse who was scoping out the race as part of a medical preparedness team.

"Where are you from?" I asked.

"We live not far from Boston," she replied.

"Oh interesting. May I ask where you work?"

"I work at St. Elizabeth's."

My breath caught. She mentioned she'd been there for many years.

"By any chance did you know Dr. Joe Stetz?" I inquired.

"I sure did!," and she went on to ask me about how I knew him.

We shared stories and our eyes filled with tears. She told me

---

that Joe injured his hand changing the oil in his car and was devastated that he could no longer practice surgery. She shared that he was looking forward to retirement having time to read books, enjoy his grandchild and ride horses. His legacy as a father and grandfather lives on in the hearts of all who were blessed to know him.

Bernie Siegel became what he affectionately calls my Chosen Dad or CD. He has become a Chosen Dad to many, like myself, who were abused and abandoned and who lost faith in ourselves. Disease manifested in our bodies and Bernie coaches us to reparent ourselves with his wisdom and guidance. We have had this beautiful relationship since the 1980's when a nurse first introduced me to his ground breaking work in the field of mind/body medicine.

After I sent him my recent book, "Hope is a Garden: Poems and Essays From the 2020 Pandemic" he sent me an email blessing me and asking me if I'd been on his radio show to share it. I've had many interviews through the years but our conversation on Dreamvisions 7 Radio deeply touched my heart and soul. He was so proud of what I had created with the Divine and his love poured forth from his heart to me. His books fill our home and his meditations are lullabies that we listen to before drifting off to sleep.

During the pandemic we have all learned, "Tomorrow is never promised. Don't wait to tell someone how you feel." I sent Bernie a Father's Day card this year. Much to my surprise, he sent me a card back to me blessing me and letting me know I am now a BD = Bonus Daughter. He is going to be 89 years young in October and I cherish every moment we share together. It was such a powerful healing moment for me this Father's Day Weekend.

In years past, I would quickly scroll past photos and Father's Day posts just wanting to 'make it through' the day. The pandemic has been a great force for transformation and growth. I am excited to celebrate Father's Day sharing those who have been like a father to me, being blessed with a husband who has been a wonderful father to our twins and to share all the feels on Father's Day 2021.

"Summer has a flavor like no other. Always fresh and simmered in sunshine." ~Oprah

Last summer we did the very best we could to savor the season that everyone in New England looks forward to. We dined al fresco in our yard either grilling or supporting local restaurants with take out. We explored new running routes in our neighborhood and played in our sprinkler. There were no trips to the beach and no Cape Cod getaways where we would lounge by outdoor pools after a morning run or having a race-vacation where we would meet up with all of our running friends. There was no dining at a restaurant because of very limited seating capacity and the metrics indicated that the risk of infection from COVID-19 was quite high.

This weekend marked the beginning of summer and coincidentally Tom's vacation.

Because of Juneteenth, Tom had Friday off. We spent the morning relaxing together as Ruth Anne prepared for an interview for her "come back job" post brain injury secondary to an autoimmune response to an untreated infection. She was hired on the spot! We had planned to do take out to kick off summer and Tom's vacation but, since we had so much to celebrate, we looked for dining out options with outdoor dining.

I wanted to be near water but we decided downtown Boston on the first weekend of summer post-COVID-19 in Boston would be too crowded for us. To ensure outside dining at Legal Seafood in Chestnut Hill, we decided an early dinner would be best. They do not take reservations for outdoor seating.

As good fortune would have it, we had a table overlooking the Pond where I was able to satisfy my desire to dine overlooking water.

"Welcome back!" One of our favorite Legal Seafood Restaurant waitresses greeted us with a huge smile.

—

It was an emotional moment for all of us. We chatted for a few minutes and the trauma of the past 15 months started to melt away. It was a bit surreal to be eating dinner out at a restaurant and for Ruth Anne getting ready to go to work again. Talk about resilience!

Since Legal Seafood was sold to new owners during the pandemic, the dishes had a different flair to them. What a treat to savor delicious food with impeccable service including the new manager personally serving our dishes to ensure they arrived right out of the kitchen. We usually do not have dessert but since there was so much to celebrate we opted for Bonbons. When she brought the check she told us that the Bonbons were complimentary.

I feel as though we have been in a time warp as we emerge from the pandemic. Having Hannah as our waitress at Legal had all the feels of being in a time warp where nothing yet everything changed.

On Saturday and Monday we went to do our 5K at the Sugar Bowl in South Boston. One of the things I missed most last summer was being able to run by the ocean. (Are you sensing that I'm a water kind of gal?)

On Monday we packed an after run picnic and spent time at the beach for the first time since the summer of 2019. What a treat to come home with sun kissed skin and 'tan' lines (which may be read as sunburned lines despite using sunscreen SPF 30), sand between our toes and salt lines on our skin from when we went into the ocean.

Because it was a weekday there was lots of room on the beach and, except for a few people wearing masks, there were no reminders that COVID-19 had swept through the city leaving deaths and devastating loss in its wake. A year ago it was hard to imagine we'd be able to ever enjoy these summer time scenes again. Ever since the diagnosis of Post-Polio Syndrome, I have practiced an attitude of gratitude. My appreciation for simple pleasures like a run around Pleasure Bay and time on the beach has deepened beyond measure since COVID-19.

A Trip to the Beach

Feel the freedom in your body
feel the freedom in your life
slowly now releasing
the past 15 months of strife.

Bring compassion, love and kindness
to the stress we've all lived through
take time allow for healing
savor sunshine skies of blue.

Emerging from the trauma
a different world we all now face
like a newborn baby from the womb
wrap yourself in tenderness and grace.

The road that we have traveled
one we never had before
miraculously we found our way
strengthened to our core.

May we be blessed with ease and peace
one toe in water we gingerly move ahead
may well-being and good health now reign
letting go of fear and dread.

May lessons from the darkest times
transform to love and light
resilience, courage, hope renewed
a change in tide is now in sight.

"There is no timestamp on trauma. There isn't a formula that you can insert yourself into to get from horror to healed. Be patient. Take up space. Let your journey be the balm." ~Dawn Serra

It seems as if we went from being in lockdown and restrictions to party time in Copley Square in Boston with a Donna Summer Disco Party. Of course I am fully aware that it was a slow almost tortuous 15 months of uncertainty, but once May 29th happened and all the restrictions were lifted, there was a shift in our lives again as abrupt as when the lockdown order went into effect on March 15 and Governor Baker declared a State of Emergency in Massachusetts.

I don't know about you but I have a little whiplash going from hearing stern warnings to people for gatherings at the beach last summer and businesses and restaurants adhering to strict restrictions because of COVID-19, to seeing a dance party in the street, runners swarming Heartbreak Hill to train for the 2021 Boston Marathon, traffic jams and planning for longer times to get from Point A to Point B. I feel as though I should be able to just jump back in to be in the flow of life again but I find myself at a bit of a loss.

I find myself experiencing the residuals from the trauma of the past 16 months with free floating anxiety and at times fatigue. I know I am not alone in these feelings as I read various articles written by people who are experiencing similar feelings. Juxtaposed with the anxiety and fatigue are feelings of intense joy and excitement to be able to experience in person connection with family and friends, do packet stuffing for the Boston Marathon and go beyond Brookline, Massachusetts to dine, to play and to experience the fullness of life again. We experienced having our hair done and going for chiropractic and acupuncture with a deeper appreciation than before the pandemic.

While we were blessed during the pandemic with Tom's job security and having our health, there were moments of intense stress. Life became a challenge as we navigated supermarkets, lived life behind masks and hands were raw from repeated hand washing. Tom and Ruth Anne had to have multiple COVID-19 tests because of work and school. Tom's job had a hiring freeze. In the wake of the pandemic and work/family stress, several people gave their notice. We experienced the collective trauma of the pandemic and the political scene in the US. It was infectious stress to see our friends experience being small business owners or working in high risk jobs. We all felt we were teetering on the brink of total disaster; a hallmark of trauma. Gratitude, meditation and prayer, love and faith were our anchors to navigate the turbulent times.

Fortunately, we can now create a space for healing as the waters of the tsunami of the pandemic and the intense political and economic climate begin to recede. While some may seemingly jump back into the flow of life, it's important to honor how we each approach this time of healing from the trauma that we have all experienced.

In the Flow

When life comes to a screeching halt
frozen in time
tightness tension
worry lines mar terrain
energy wanes to a trickle.

When paralyzed by fear
faith edged out
come back from the edge.

As danger subsides
slowly thawing
torch of divine love lights the way
Source tenderly melting pain.

Haltingly I return to life
here and now
all there is
ebb and flow with the tide
no more precious stolen moments.

Smiling
tears of relief flow
heart swells with gratitude
getting back in the swim of life
in the flow
faith all is well.

...a phrase that President Biden used before we turned the corner of the pandemic. He reminded us that we'd come so far but needed to go the distance before letting up on safety precautions and the need to get vaccinated. We continue to go the distance as we emerge from the pandemic ever mindful that we need to take steps to ensure we are part of the prevention of COVID-19 instead of the spread.

During our Father's Day conversation with our son, I momentarily forgot about COVID-19. We were making plans for celebrating the twins 34th birthday together. There were reminders that we still have more miles to go before we can cross the finish line of the pandemic. He hasn't been able to see a dentist and his partner Michelle hasn't seen her physician because of the pandemic. We were also mindful about how things have changed. In pre-COVID-19 times, Autumn would not hesitate getting on a bus and coming into Boston but now he and Michelle need to work out logistics to manage a visit while tending to their farm and animals. None of us is ready to eat indoors at a restaurant yet. It was reassuring to hear Gayle King say that she was anxious about going to the theater when they covered the story of Bruce Springsteen's show reopening Broadway for the first time in 16 months.

My daughter and I have wanted to go for a swim but when we found out being fully vaccinated was not a requirement at our Town pool, we decided to wait. We are so close to the finish line!

I've been reflecting on words and phrases that we didn't know before the pandemic and the emotions that are associated with this new vocabulary:

Socially distanced
Mask up
Fully vaxed
Quarantine
Lockdown
Phased Reopening

mRNA technology
Variants

There were some incredibly rough miles during these past 16 months and there is still some uncertainty on the road ahead, but I fervently believe that we will go the distance in leaving the pandemic in the past.

I've also been reflecting on my own journey of transformation and the analogy of life being a marathon not a sprint; a phrase often used by epidemiologists and leaders as they reference ending the pandemic and one that is apropos to my life in the wake of childhood paralytic polio and trauma. Nobody would have judged me for accepting the diagnosis and prognosis of Post-Polio Syndrome after all the challenges I endured. I could have decided that leaving my award-winning career as a VA social worker and accepting the progression of accelerated aging as a result of the initial polio virus would be the finish line of my journey in this lifetime.

Instead, I dared to go the distance and defy the diagnosis and my past to heal my life.

In Massachusetts, we are blessed with a very high vaccination rate. We are still mindful that we have not yet crossed the finish line, arms thrust in the air feeling victorious that the miles of the pandemic are behind us. We are close. My hope and prayer is that every individual chooses to dare to go the distance in caring for themselves, our communities and our world choosing health and well-being, love, kindness, forgiveness and compassion. My hope is that everyone can respect each other's choices knowing that not everyone can or should receive the vaccine. As long as we honor ourselves and do everything we can to promote the health and well-being of ourselves and our communities, we can all go the distance together!

My body's reaction to emerging from the pandemic has taken me off guard. It's a time of great paradox. While there are moments when it feels as if the pandemic never happened and we went from March 12, 2020 to May 29, 2021 experiencing a kind of time warp to things being "normal again," there is a cloud of fear with the news of the Delta variant and lockdowns happening in other parts of the world. There is joy and celebration on this Fourth of July as we celebrate freedom from COVID-19, yet I am experiencing a sense of awkwardness and trepidation as we move beyond these past 16 months.

After the 2nd vaccine, I experienced a lot of joint pain and muscle spasms. Was it a response to the vaccine or perhaps a reaction to all the stress and body flashbacks from polio and trauma I endured in childhood? Regardless of the cause, meditation and visualization helped to ease the pain.

This past week, with plans for Tom to return to the office {hopefully in a hybrid model}, Ruth Anne getting ready to work part-time and be on campus in late August, and the 50th anniversary of when my father ended his life after brutalizing us in the summer of 1971, my emotions expressed themselves through my body. I experienced a flood of emotions that I could not find words for which is highly unusual for me.

I listened as my body spoke expressing the trauma past and present in a myriad of ways. In my meditations, I focused on calm, peace, ease and freedom.

This morning I said to my body, "Okay. I hear you. Enough!" Rather than focus on the physicality of what was happening in my body, I thought, "What do you want to create? You've got to focus your thoughts on what is going to shift your body chemistry rather than maintain the stress."

—

During my meditation I took deep breaths and I heard Spirit speak the words, 'You deserve to feel and be well. You deserve to be free from experiencing the trauma in your body. Feel Source's Love in every cell.' I knew it was incumbent upon me to feel and find my freedom and be bold in claiming my health and well-being.

The following poem flowed through me after I finished my meditation:

Be Bold

Dare to believe
you are worthy of a wonderful life
imagination opens door to infinite possibilities
hope and healing a breath away.
Emboldened by Source's Love
Sorcerer co-creating
conjuring ease
even in midst of strife
peace treaty
bold to be free
freedom from fear.

Unfreezing
blazing a new trail
pathways of light
dispersing clouds of darkness
despairing depressing thoughts
whisked away
negatives developed
reveal Truth.

Be bold
daring to be joyful
smiling from depths of soul
believe in birthright
let freedom ring!

I felt my heart open and only whispers from the symptoms that were plaguing me lingered. I felt more steady and calm and know that I need to draw from this state of being as we move forward emerging from the pandemic.

"The secret to happiness is freedom, and the secret to freedom is courage." ~Thucydides

It takes courage and being bold to face whatever is keeping us from experiencing our natural state of joy, happiness and well-being. When we do we experience life as Source intended us to.

Let freedom ring as we enjoy this Fourth of July free from the constraints of the pandemic feeling deep gratitude for how far we've come in the past year.

"The only time you should look back in life is to see how far you've come." ~Kevin Hart

As "Hail to the Chief" played, President Joseph R. Biden Jr. walked on the red carpet with a spring in his 78 year old step to deliver his Fourth of July remarks at the White House BBQ with essential workers and military families. He reminded us that we are declaring our independence from a deadly virus. Invited guests stood against a backdrop of red, white and blue balloons in the trees on the White House Lawn.

Looking back to 1776, he was quick to point out that our country was fashioned out of the power of an idea and now we have the power of science. As he celebrated America and, that we the people are back together again, the patriotic thing one can do is to vaccinate yourself for your loved ones, community and country. He reminded us that we never want to be where we were a year ago today. He celebrated how the virus no longer controls our lives or paralyzes our nation and it is now within our power to make sure it never does that again. He was quick to point out that putting the pandemic behind us and resurrecting the economy has been one of the most remarkable achievements in American history but in the midst of joy we know the heartache of loss that so many have endured from the virus and from other tragedies during this past year.

It was such an inspiring way to kick off our July 4th Celebration. We had our traditional BBQ Chicken, grilled potatoes and salad. Over dinner, we reflected on where we were a year ago and how far we have come in our own lives, and as a country. Ruth Anne was quick to point out that a year ago we didn't even know if "the other guy" was going to serve a second term. The streets were silent. We wore masks wherever we went and while we focused on gratitude, love, performing acts of kindness and compassion, there was a constant hum of fear, anxiety and uncertainty. There were no Fourth of July celebrations and we all did the best we could to get through that time of darkness.

———

The last time we saw fireworks was on January 20, 2021 at the Inauguration of President Biden. We were overcome with emotion then, and this Fourth of July we were overcome with emotion as we watched "A Capital Fourth" and The Boston Pops live concert from Tanglewood.

Keith Lockhart was overcome with emotion as he welcomed the audience and thanked them for being there. Sixteen months after no performances, he shared the emotions we all have come to know; the mixture of relief, joy and grief for what we had to endure.

There was no live audience for "A Capital Fourth" but Vanessa Williams and 'surprise host' Kermit the Frog introduced the musicians and were later joined by Christopher Jackson for a live performance to cap off the concert before a 25 minute fireworks display over Washington. Macy's fireworks lit up the New York City skyline. Crowds gathered on Boston Common to witness a fireworks display as the Pops played the traditional 1812 Overture in Tanglewood.

It was a stunning Fourth of July celebration with the theme America is Back Together Again. The themes of unity, freedom, justice and all the principles of our Founding Fathers rang out across the land in song and celebration.

When we look back on a year ago when we were held captive by a virus and our President, we realize how incredibly far we've come. As President Biden said, it is a time of hope, promise and possibility.

With sweltering summer heat, we've experienced intense thunderstorms this past week in New England. After the first set of storms moved through, I looked to the skies to see if we could find a rainbow. We were treated to the beautiful light of the setting sun and the sweet scent of summer air after the rain but no rainbow.

The next day we had more thunderstorms. Would we see a rainbow?

It was still raining as the sun came out. I peered out the living room window and the vague colors of the rainbow slowly emerged against the backdrop of grey sky. I shouted to Ruth Anne to come quickly. There was going to be a rainbow. We grabbed our iPhones and snapped pictures. When I went to upload the photos, I saw that Tom had been stopped at a light on his way to Trader Joe's and sent me photos of rainbows on Beacon Street. The Facebook newsfeed was filled with photos of rainbows. It was as though the Universe was sending us a sign of the impending end of the pandemic. It was a very Noah's Ark kind of moment; a powerful sign of Divine Love and a reminder to keep the faith especially through the storms.

Were it not for the powerful storms and darkness, how could we experience rainbows? And how could we possibly experience the profound heart opening sense of grace and gratitude when we make the rainbow connection.

The Rainbow Connection

Do you still feel the thrill
after a thunderstorm
wind dies down
sun shines while rain pours
look up
faded colors transform
vibrancy emerges out of the ethers
suddenly it appears
covenant of Divine Love.

A stirring in my soul
childlike delight
a blessing
standing in pouring rain
baptized
capturing its image
before it fades
leaves lasting imprint
on my heart and soul

I found it
the rainbow connection
tethering me to infinite beauty
of Divine love and light!

"Life is a marathon, not a sprint: pace yourself accordingly." ~Amby Burfoot

Summer is usually a time to kick back and savor a slower pace. Of course we didn't quite anticipate that last summer our pace would be slowed to a crawl but pandemic life forced us to slow down, notice things we might have allowed to rush by us and feel immensely grateful for health and simple pleasures. The pace of life has picked up this summer with plans to return to in person work and school, signing up for races, and the once empty spaces surrounding magnets on our refrigerator are now filled with event invitations.

I am thrilled that we don't need masks in most settings, can safely socialize and life has resumed with activities we enjoy, but it seems as though the pace has quickened beyond what I have become accustomed to during these past 16 months.

One of the ways that I manage feeling overwhelmed is to push my pace on a run. Saturday, Ruth Anne and Tom paced me on our Jamaica Plain run. It wasn't planned. It evolved from the inside. Despite picking up the pace on our run, we made sure to pause to savor the beauty around us.

By the end of the run my mood was lifted and I enjoyed that feeling of being spent after a good run. We haven't been racing for the past 16 months {and I am still undecided about whether or not I am going to return to racing}. There is a special feeling when you push yourself and pass people ahead of you and sweat pours even after finishing the run.

The stillness of the water helped my heart and soul to settle and the endorphins enabled my parasympathetic nervous system to kick in.

When the pace picks up and the world seems to be resuming its pre-pandemic frenzy, I can pause, breathe and get my bearings. There's no need for me to get swept along in the current. I enjoy being my only competition these days. Initially, I missed our annual races complete with what we affectionately called "race-cations". I missed hugging friends and gathering with members of our L Street Running Club. I missed challenging myself going for PR's and the thrill of Facebook feedback when I conquered the clock at a race.

As we emerge from the pandemic, everyone should find their own pace just as we do when we toe the starting line of a race. There are no judgments for what choices people make and what suits them mind, body and soul. I do want to cherish the soul lessons we've learned and preserve some of the habits we developed during the pandemic. Some may choose to go out fast when the gun goes off and stay out in front resuming pre-pandemic activities at a pre-pandemic pace. Others may hang in the middle of the pack keeping a steady pace finding their way along the course. And still others, like me, will be at the back of the pack finding my way into a new rhythm of life emerging from the pandemic remembering that life is a marathon, not a sprint and to pace myself accordingly.

"Anyone who thinks that sunshine is pure happiness has never run in the rain." ~Anonymous

July is looking to be a record-breaking month for rain this year. As sweltering heat, fires and drought plague the West Coast, Boston is on record to be the wettest July since 1872. In the first 12 days, July is the third wettest July ever recorded from 1872 until now. I give thanks every day that we have an Administration addressing the crisis of climate change partnering with the global stage to heal Mother Earth and fiercely working to end the pandemic.

Before COVID-19, we would have been spending more hours in the gym rationalizing that a swim, treadmill or elliptical workout could be traded for a running day. As we emerge from the pandemic, we have not renewed a gym membership. I woke up at 4:30am {with a little help from our beloved cat Jamie jumping on me asking read that as demanding to be fed} as the rain pelted our window panes. I focused my intention on the rain easing up enough for us to get in our run. I fell back to sleep until 6:45am when the alarm went off.

Still pouring...

It was a rest day for Ruth Anne so the decision was up to Tom and me about whether or not we would get out the door for a run. At least it wasn't cold as it was on Memorial Day Weekend. We had done strength training on Sunday so we could not do another strength training session. I could not bear the thought of heading to the basement for a treadmill run in summer.

We donned lightweight layers, a water belt to protect our phones and to hydrate, and off we went!

We smiled and laughed embracing the elements. We weren't sure if the Reservoir would be flooded but once we got there it looked like

---

72

we could run around the path. By the time we got to our halfway mark, the puddles on the other side of the Reservoir were impossible to wade through. We reversed course to finish our 5K.

"Feet soaking wet - check." Tom commented at one point.

"Ooh I'm not there yet," I said but a short time later, my shoes and socks reached their saturation point. I made squeaking noises with each foot fall.

Although we have had many runs in the rain throughout our running career, neither one of us could remember running in a steady torrential downpour as we experienced yesterday. We fondly recalled a long run training for the Bermuda Half Marathon one year but the rain would ease up at times. The sun even came out at the end of that training run.

"I can't believe we're doing this," I said to Tom as we were on the back end of our 5K."

"I don't know many almost 70 year old people who would be out here splashing in the puddles and slogging through a 5K at 7 in the morning before breakfast."

"This is what keeps us young at heart!"

"We don't stop playing because we grow old; we grow old because we stop playing." ~George Bernard Shaw

Ruth Anne greeted us with her raincoat on as we came into the yard. She had breakfast ready for us.

On the run we strategized that we would peel off our outer layers and toss them into a trash bag, get changed upstairs and throw everything into the wash. I was in shock at how much our wet clothes weighed. "Hey that was like running in a weighted vest," I quipped.

I felt cleansed mind, body and soul inside and out. As one who has endured and overcome childhood paralytic polio and trauma, I felt deep gratitude for every rain soaked footstep!

Experiences take on richer and deeper meaning as we emerge from the pandemic. Feeling connected to nature and the Divine has taken on a sense of urgency. I couldn't bear to be confined to a treadmill when it was safe to run outside. There was a welcomed sense of unbridled freedom during the run and a feeling of being able to conquer any challenges that may come our way.

The run also inspired this poem:

Believe

Rain pounding window pane
believe
be grateful
grace is raining down.
When faith reigns
all is well
delight in puddle play
forever young.
Fret not
flood of emotions
flowing
all storms pass.
Rainwater cleanses
clearing confusion
heart beats with eager anticipation
smile of inner knowing
sun shines again.

con'tent'ment (kuhn-tent-muhnt): *The state of being mentally or emotionally satisfied with things just as they are; peace of* mind *~On line dictionary*

With all that has transpired these past 16 months, finding that sweet spot of contentment with a feeling of inner peace has been a gift; the total grace. We basked in the glow of the setting sun while dining al fresco in our yard. We took walks and discovered new running routes in our neighborhood. We had many moments of contentment being at home, playing board games and brain games, and doing jigsaw puzzles. We delighted in finding new recipes and had many hearty laughs when a recipe did not quite turn out as we had anticipated. We felt blessed and grateful that Tom was able to work from home and Ruth Anne's classes were on line to keep us safe in our bubble.

We had to adapt to wearing masks, doing only take out, not being able to swim, travel or hang out at the beaches last summer. We tested our mettle running outdoors as long as it was safe and learned how to challenge ourselves despite not having any races. A regular meditation practice focused on peace, ease, acceptance and experiencing comfort within the discomfort. As runners and runners who have run the Boston Marathon, we were able to get through those tough miles.

Emerging from the pandemic, we are faced with making choices about what events to attend. Events that we would not ordinarily give a second thought to now give us pause, especially with an uptick in cases among the unvaccinated due to the Delta variant. Going to my husband's family's house for a pool party to celebrate the graduation of the cousin who my twins grew up with would have been a pre-COVID-19 no brainer. As I saw the invitation on my refrigerator, I began experiencing a sense of unease about attending the party. Tom, Ruth Anne and I sat down to talk about it.

We received an invitation from one of Ruth Anne's friends for a "See and Sip" to celebrate the birth of her friend's son. They live in California but are returning to her friend's house so that the friends she grew up with can celebrate the baby's birth. On the invitation it states, "Kindly be fully vaccinated if you plan to attend."

My husband's cousin's family has children who are not yet of age to receive the vaccination. We have no way of knowing the vaccination status of the graduate's friends. When the pandemic first hit, my husband's cousin who is the grandmother of the graduate, had posts on her Facebook page about conflicts over masks in her apartment building. We have incredible memories of many holidays spent with my husband's family and during the pandemic reached out to reconnect with them. It's great to share in each other's lives on Facebook but as we talked, we realized a big party is not going to serve us well right now even though we are fully vaccinated. I contracted polio in one of the last polio epidemics at the age of 5. I was fully vaccinated but after playing with my friend, whose mother was not vaccinated, I contracted paralytic polio. In today's lingo, they call it a rare breakthrough case. I believe in living in love and light and not living in fear but I do respect this virus and its variants and want to put myself in situations that will promote health and well-being.

It's easy to have FOMO - a fear of missing out on an afternoon of swimming in the pool at my husband's family's house, eating and reminiscing enjoying the love of family. I recently saw this:

JOMO - noun - a feeling of contentment with one's own pursuits and activities, without worrying over the possibility of missing out on what others may be doing. ~Anil Dash

We could have made up a reason about why we were not going to attend like Tom had to be on call or his back was bothering him and we couldn't make the trip but we all felt it was important to be truth tellers. We put a graduation card and check in the mail and sent our warmest regards and best wishes.

We will go to the "See and Sip." It will be a mostly outdoor event where everyone will be fully vaccinated. We experienced a lot of angst earlier this week. We realized it was the combination of Tom's return to the office one day a week beginning NOW and the conflict we experienced around Saturday's family event. I'm sure the seemingly never ending days of rain did not help.

After a lot of meditation and discussion, we were able to settle down and once again find that sweet spot of contentment which is perfect as we get ready to head into the weekend with the summer's early dismissal on Fridays at 3pm.

Whenever we find ourselves veering off course, we know we can take a breath and trust that we will always return to that sweet spot of contentment and gratitude.

Contentment

When turmoil of world roils
thoughts boiling over
confinement
why
whining
wishing
wanting

STOP

gratitude unlocks door
opens heart
deep breath
transforms complaining

Look around
notes to self
simple pleasures
quiet evening at home
sumptuous summer fruit
sweet fragrance after the rain
reunion hugs
taste of first snowflakes
icicles like diamonds on trees
splendor of autumn leaves.

Piece by piece
weaving together
tapestry of peace and contentment.

Contentment is not the fulfillment of what you want, but the realization of how much you already have. ~Anonymous

Keep Hope Alive

I posted a photo of swans swimming together from our morning run earlier in the week. We received a lot of comments on our Facebook post including "not ducks in a row but swans," "beautiful", and "awesome photo."

Last night, Bernie Siegel commented, "no competition, unity."

I replied, "yes nature is so amazing . I just felt my heart and soul settle with your comment."

As I fell asleep last night, I reflected on the serenity of this moment and when I finished my morning meditation, wrote this poem:

Unity

Elegant
epitome of grace
swans serenely swimming
instincts guide
poised and peaceful
a chorus line orchestrated by Divine
for heart and soul's delight.

Powerful moment
movement as One
how we all can be
Being in harmony
rhythm of nature
flowing
growing
reflecting true essence
borne from God
breeding a new world order.

When we look to nature we discover our true nature. As Bernie was quick to point out, there was no competition among the swans.

I am taken back to when vaccines first became available and everyone was in competition with everyone else to get their shot. Ironically, now, there is more than enough supply but not enough people eager to get vaccinated.

May we all be in the rhythm and flow of life in unity heading in the same direction with grace and serenity.

"Enjoy the journey; embrace the detours." ~Anonymous

I've recently encountered a lot of detours on my runs and on the road of life. I was on a run around the Reservoir when a detour sign appeared. I turned to Ruth Anne and said, "Well what shall we do?"

We came up with a plan to go into a familiar path under a canopy of trees. We would go to the halfway mark of our 5K and return the same way we ran to get to the halfway point.

It started to rain; nothing like the downpour Tom and I experienced last week but a steady rain. The canopy of leaves caught the rain keeping us relatively dry. When we emerged from our detour, the rain stopped.

Ever since the diagnosis of Post-Polio Syndrome in December of 2006, I have learned to find joy in the journey and embrace the detours. The detour of Post-Polio Syndrome led me to the most glorious destination of becoming a 2009 Boston Marathon finisher, motivational speaker, author, poet and one who shares a profound message of healing, hope and possibilities.

The 2020 pandemic was a mother lode of all detours. We were extremely blessed to maintain our health and well-being through it all. We thought that after we were all vaccinated we could resume activities and see friends without any trepidation. We are extremely fortunate in Massachusetts to have a high vaccination rate and a relatively low infection rate but the vaccination rate has dramatically slowed and there is an "uptick" in cases that is of concern to public health officials.

I focus on accentuating the positive, releasing fears and trusting in the Divine, believing in my health and well-being and in the health and well-being of my loved ones. When I meditate, I send out well-being to all Beings. I know the power of the mind/body connection and harness it to boost my immune system and continue to heal my life from the once devastating effects of paralytic polio and trauma.

This new "uptick" in cases in Massachusetts and around the country have given our family and me pause. The news that came out of the CDC that if you are fully vaccinated, you can go about your lives with ease and no masks was a cause for celebration. But given what's happening, one wonders if they may have moved forward too quickly with their advice. I know they were basing it on available data. They used it as a motivator to encourage people to get vaccinated based on the data at that time. We were not about to book a trip that would require traveling by air but we did book a trip to New York City. The words of Lin-Manuel Miranda on the Tonight Show with Jimmy Fallon are now echoing once more. As Jimmy Fallon and he were talking about the excitement of Broadway's reopening, he said *"And it's all depending, right? It depends on how safe people feel returning to the theater and people continuing to get vaccinated…"*

We know about the power of belief and trust in the efficacy of the vaccines we received. Our concerns lie with people who are unvaccinated and the risk of breakthrough infection which is what happened to me during the last polio epidemic. Even if that were to happen we know we would be fine but why take the risk right now? We have returned to hand washing and masks indoors and making choices based on our tolerance for risk, weighing the benefits versus risk of our choices. We are taking life day by day which is truly the only way to be. We are aware that life can and does change on a dime.

We'll continue to enjoy life with an attitude of gratitude undeterred by any detours that may come our way. The beautiful destination we arrive at is the gift of the present moment where we have everything we could possibly need and more.

"When we are no longer able to change a situation, we are challenged to change ourselves." ~Victor Frankl

It can be very easy to feel discouraged by the latest news about "breakthrough" cases of COVID-19 in vaccinated persons and an overall uptick in cases for unvaccinated persons. Uncertainty of the trajectory of the pandemic once again brings great concern to public health officials and to the general population. The only thing I can control is what choices I make about the risks I choose to take when going out and choosing my perspective. My family and I made the choice to get vaccinated.

We are now choosing to wear a mask indoors.

I absolutely loved this editorial from CNN written by Comilla Sasson, MD, Ph.D. She compared navigating COVID-19 to being on an airplane:

When we get to cruising altitude, the seatbelt light turns off and we can now move freely aboard the aircraft. But sometimes we hit turbulence. When the pilot comes on the speakers and says, "time to get back in your seats and put your seat belt on," we (most of us at least), find our seats, put on our seatbelts, and brace ourselves for a rocky ride.

When we put our seatbelts on, do we ask ourselves, why didn't the pilots, flight attendants or air control predict this? Do we question the credibility, reliability, or intentions of our flight crew? Nope. We understand that things can change quickly, and we must adjust to the conditions. There is a reason for what we are doing.

She goes on to say, *"Well, COVID-19 is the biggest, scariest pandemic plane ride, and the entire world is currently on it together. When we go into lockdowns, restrict travel, and mandate masks and other prevention strategies, health care and public health officials, along with government workers, make their decisions based on the data they have, with conditions changing quickly, in order to keep the public safe. Vaccines came out and are ridiculously effective in preventing people from becoming hospitalized as a result of COVID-19. We had hit that beautiful cruising altitude in our pandemic plane ride, where we could all take a breath, literally and figuratively, and take off our masks, see family & friends again, and reopen businesses and schools.*

But the vaccines are not a silver bullet. We can still get COVID-19. But the chances are dramatically lower that we will get COVID-19 if we are vaccinated, and even if we do, it will be a mild case that does not require hospitalization. What we didn't and couldn't predict, is how quickly COVID-19 itself changes, how much of the world remains unvaccinated, and that this novel coronavirus, which no one had heard of or had to treat just 24 months ago, would cause these crazy, unpredictable, turbulent conditions.

Tom and I ran in a torrential downpour last week. Our perspective kept us moving mile after mile until we hit the 5K mark which was our goal. It was relatively warm outside. Soon, snow and ice will return, so we wanted to enjoy being outdoors without layers upon layers of clothing. We are healthy and enjoy our unplugged time together. When Ruth Anne and I were in the middle of a run and it started to drizzle, we had perspective that at least it was not the torrential downpour on our previous run.

After last year's pandemic experience, we have a very different perspective on this year's uptick in COVID-19 cases. There is hope with the vaccine and knowledge that with masking, vaccination, social distancing and good hygiene as well as investing in our individual health and well-being, we can and will end the pandemic. We flattened the curve and we can do it again.

A new language emerged last year that included phrases such as mask up, social distancing, fully vaxed, lockdown, quarantine, phased re-openings and supply chain shortages. As we emerge from the pandemic, I see phrases now such as Post-Pan (We Hope) and Quasi-Pandemic. A year ago, those phrases were not even on our radar. There is no State of Emergency splashed at the top of every page across our home delivered Boston Globe.

That space on our bookcase for masks just in case is now once again filled with masks and are part of our regular laundry.

The risk of contracting COVID-19 as a fully vaccinated family is extremely low and we are keeping that risk low by re-instituting wearing masks and being mindful of what social activities we plan to be a part of.

Last year we had to wear masks all the time and the risk of contracting COVID-19 was quite high limiting our choices of what we could do and where we could go.

Is it disheartening that officials declared the pandemic over and we were set free to live our lives only to see the metrics moving in a direction indicating that the pandemic is not yet over?

Of course it is! But I prefer to keep everything in perspective living with an attitude of gratitude and seeing how far we've come from where we were last year at this time.

Vulnerability

Sharing tears and fears
tearing off veil
revealing true self
fullness of human experience
embraced by unconditional love
acceptance
courage unbridled by COVID-19
urgency and hunger
true connection
nowhere and no need to hide.

Hard conversations
truth telling
beauty in raw emotions
holding sacred space for each other
tenderness
undam emotions
flooding heart with love
transforming damnation
forgiveness and gratitude
releasing decades of pent up pain
emerging from shadows of former self
crisis an opportunity
excitement
exploring
bathing wounds
feel the heal
a brave new world
riding waves
only certainty in uncertainty
companions exploring lighting the way
emerging
transforming
healing path
paved with Divine Love.

"Hope: Never Underestimate the power of hope. Hope fuels us with the energy and courage to go forward." ~Adele Basheer

It is very unlike me to feel depressed, frustrated, angry and hopeless about what's happening with the pandemic. I let fear take over on Sunday when we were going to go to the beach. I asked Tom to turn around after we drove halfway to South Boston. A year ago we were able to adapt to circumstances knowing what precautions to take to keep ourselves and our loved ones healthy. It was challenging but after a few months found a rhythm to life practicing gratitude and optimism feeling hope and faith deep in our hearts.

After we were fully vaccinated, we knew it would be some time before the pandemic was in the rear view mirror but when we received the all clear from the CDC, the White House, and Governor Baker, we breathed a collective sigh of relief. We did not rush out to book a trip that required a plane ride or head indoors to eat at a restaurant but felt wonderful to have that freedom to choose. We were stopped in our tracks when the news of rising cases and hot spots even in our state of Massachusetts, with one of the highest vaccination rates in the country, made the headlines. Reports of 'breakthrough' cases were on the rise.

When the news first broke about the pandemic, I wasn't frightened of becoming ill. I experienced the trauma of being in lockdown and seeing the world and our lives come to a screeching halt. I focused on health and well-being. I have total confidence in the vaccines and my immune system but could not shake my feelings of fear and discomfort. Perhaps it was coming from my experience during the polio epidemic. Tom and Ruth Anne were supportive, loving and kind and we spent the day at home on Sunday. I couldn't seem to find my way out of my funk.

After having a miserable day on Sunday, I focused Monday morning's meditation on turning the tide of my attitude and mindset. I knew that the energy I was putting out was attracting negative posts to my social media newsfeed and creating an atmosphere of unease in the household. After listening to David Hamilton's Tibetan Sound Bowl Meditation, I felt refreshed and decided that I needed a booster shot of hope, optimism and happiness. I asked Ruth Anne if she would like to do our run in South Boston after breakfast. She was thrilled and so was I!

It was a sultry summer's day and it probably wasn't smart of me to push my pace but I needed to get those endorphins kicking and feel my strength and resilience resounding throughout my entire body. Shortly after we set out on our run, we bumped into one of the members of our L Street Running Club family. Ruth Anne and I had a delightful conversation expressing our gratitude and appreciation for all the good things in our lives. We reflected on how perhaps there could have been a slower reopening and removal of the mask mandate, but there's no turning back on what is.

"I really don't know why it is that all of us are so committed to the sea, except I think it's because in addition to the fact that the sea changes, and the light changes, and ships change, it's because we all came from the sea. And it is an interesting biological fact that all of us have in our veins the exact same percentage of salt in our blood that exists in the ocean, and, therefore, we have salt in our blood, in our sweat, in our tears. We are tied to the ocean. And when we go back to the sea - whether it is to sail or to watch it - we are going back from whence we came." ~JFK

A year ago at this time we couldn't go anywhere near South Boston given the high infection rate in the City and would have had to wear a mask if we did. We deeply breathed in the sea air taking special note of summer's beauty. By the end of our 5K we were soaked with sweat and filled with joy.

My newsfeed and the news took a noticeable shift. Vaccine mandates are being implemented. There is a lot of peer pressure for vaccination and people are masking up in public. My booster shot of hope was working and I was able to turn the tide of feeling hopeful again despite appearances to the contrary.

Turning the Tide

Yesterday so filled with fear stumbling lost my way
clearing out the cobwebs I begin a brand new day.
Hope was buried in the darkness of headlines grim and drear
a shift a change in attitude as close as heart so dear.
Connecting with the Source of all Love must now prevail
a tender touch extending through adversity we can sail.
Though the waters may be rocky we hold still safe inside
Divine with all its wisdom steadily is our guide.

When thinking that the coast is clear and storms come into view
unwavering faith beyond appearances will always see us through.
A GPS a compass to navigate the night
calm the waves of queasiness eradicate all fright.
Standing at the helm of life strength rising from the soul
Creator deep within us current flowing feeling whole.
Rising up to meet all challenges seas will be calm once more
look out to the horizon we'll make it safely back to shore.

"Peace. It does not mean to be in a place where there is no noise, trouble or hard work. It means to be in the midst of those things and still be calm in your heart." ~Unknown

I've been focusing on peace in my meditations and as I go about my day. As I cycle through moments of anxiety, I take deep breaths and focus on what I have control over and what I don't have control over. I found myself riding the wild roller coaster of the tale of two pandemics. In Burlington, Vermont people are at crowded bars, dancing the night away and quoted in the news as feeling fearless and free. Their state has the highest vaccination rate and lowest infection rate in the country. Massachusetts is close behind Vermont in its vaccination rate but recently has seen clusters of outbreaks. There are 5 counties in Massachusetts with high and substantial transmission rates.

The Centers for Disease Control and Prevention updated its masking guidelines on Tuesday, recommending vaccinated individuals wear masks indoors where community transmission levels are classified as high or substantial. I've had to limit my exposure to news stories and am just checking in to see what the latest mandates are for our area. Our family has made the decision to mask up when we are indoors and stocked up on a new supply of masks. While I feel twinges of sadness, anger and frustration when I look at my bookshelf where, for a brief moment in time, there was space with only one mask per person 'just in case', I know it does not serve me to dwell in the space of "what if they only waited to lift restrictions until more people were vaccinated." There is no going back. We can only go forward as best we know how, once again navigating unknowns and uncertainty in the wacky world of COVID-19.

I do know for certain that we have taken every measure we can to ensure a healthy lifestyle mind, body and soul focusing especially on our mental health and well-being. Fear and anxiety, and listening to the 'latest' data which are constantly in flux serve only to suppress the immune system. Finger pointing and blame, "What if's" and "If only's " wreak havoc with our body's chemistry.

Peace, on the other hand, allows for the production of the body's natural chemistry that is set to bring balance, healing and a strong immune response. While at times it feels as though the weight of the pandemic is bearing down on us again, it is vital to find joy, laughter, lightness and ease in our lives. Even if it is not happening in the moment, imagining those feelings pulls us out of the vortex of darkness in the moment.

I received this message from Telecharge today:

Broadway is all about gathering together and sharing in the experience of live theatre. The theatre industry is committed to the health and safety of all members of the Broadway community— theatre employees, production staff, cast, and audience members.

To ensure the safety of everyone in the theatre, the following policies will be in place for your performance:

Order #:88589048
Performance Date: 10/3/2021 3:00:00 PM

MASKS REQUIRED
For performances through October 31, 2021:
Everyone in the theatre must wear acceptable face coverings at all times, including during the show, except while eating or drinking in designated locations. All face coverings must cover the nose and mouth and comply with the CDC guidelines for acceptable face coverings.

VACCINATIONS REQUIRED
For performances through October 31, 2021:
Guests will need to be fully vaccinated with an FDA or WHO authorized vaccine in order to attend a show and must show proof of vaccination at their time of entry into the theatre with their valid ticket. "Fully vaccinated" means the performance date you are

attending must be:

at least 14 days after your second dose of an FDA or WHO authorized two dose COVID-19 vaccine, or

at least 14 days after your single dose of an FDA or WHO authorized single dose COVID-19 vaccine.

The only exception to the above will be for guests under the age of 12, or those who need reasonable accommodations due to a medical condition or sincerely held religious belief. Guests requesting an exemption must provide proof of at least one of the following, in addition to properly wearing a mask inside the building:

negative COVID-19 PCR test taken within 72 hours of the performance, or

negative COVID-19 rapid antigen test taken within 6 hours of the performance.

Guests may present proof of vaccination or a negative test on paper or a smartphone. For example, New York State residents, or anyone who received a COVID-19 vaccine in New York State, may present proof through the use of the Excelsior Pass.

In addition to proof of vaccination, all guests 18 years or older must also present a government-issued photo ID, such as a driver's license or passport. Guests under 18 may also use a school photo ID. Guests under 12 must be accompanied by an adult who meets the above requirements.

Guests who do not comply with these policies will be denied entry or asked to leave the theatre. If you feel you cannot follow these guidelines, visit your ORDER STATUS page and exchange to a later date or request a refund.

We're all in this together. Thank you for being part of our community and following these new policies. We look forward to seeing you very soon. In the meantime, let us know if there's anything else we can do.

I felt tears well up in my eyes and a lump in my throat as the reality of the pandemic continues to take center stage in our lives. We decided now is just not the right time to go to the theater in New York. Wearing a mask for two and a half hours just doesn't appeal to us and part of the thrill of going to the theater is experiencing the crush of people waiting in line to get into the theater. We'd have to present a government issued photo ID along with our proof of vaccination. Wearing a mask before dining on deli, or eating Italian at Mama Mia's takes the joy out of the New York City experience.

I hearken back to Lin-Manuel Miranda's words to Jimmy Fallon when they were celebrating the re-opening of Broadway, *"It's all depending right? On vaccinations and whether or not people will feel comfortable returning to the theater."*

All of those invitations with printed out google maps for directions to different events are gone from our refrigerator. There are still lots of posts in my newsfeed of people who are traveling, dining out, going to bars and acting as if the pandemic has ended. We are going to err on the side of caution as a tale of two pandemics continues, and to focus on all we have to be grateful for.

After we cancelled our New York City trip we bought ice cream savoring the taste of summer in New England watching a glorious sunset. We held a space for our sadness and frustration while expressing what we are each grateful for.

As the scientists try to sift and sort data, and as politicians focus on what to do about the myriad challenges facing us at this time in our history, I am going to focus on being the change.

Be The Change

Wildfires raging
mood as dark as thick smoke
enveloping all in its path
virus' variant wreaking havoc

How to stop the carnage?

Tears from an open heart extinguish hopelessness
compassion and kindness fan flames of healing
turn off talking heads
turn toward each other
feel the heal.

Grateful for blessings great and small
tender moments
tending to each other's wounds
beauty of sunsets
tomatoes ripe on the vine
savor and appreciate.

Bind broken heartedness
banding together
we are one
powerful to effect change
one action creates ripples
slowly
reversing
damage we once wrought.

A Higher Authority   August 1, 2021

"All you need is faith, trust and a little pixie dust." ~Walt Disney

During these times of confusion about what all the data mean in relationship to recent outbreaks of breakthrough cases among vaccinated individuals and conflicting information about whether or not to mask up again, I like to put my faith in a higher authority.

After reading an article in the Globe about the data coming out of a study of a recent outbreak of the Delta Variant in Provincetown, I took a time out to meditate.

A commercial for Hebrew National Hot Dogs came to me. It was an old TV commercial in which the spokesman for Hebrew National Hot Dogs says that their hot dogs are kosher and exceed government standards. They answer to a higher authority.

I could easily get dizzy trying to comprehend the different data and recommendations. Instead, I turn to my higher authority to discern what my family and I need to do to remain of sound mind and body during this time. We are going to mostly stay in our bubble and mask up when we are indoors. Tom returns to the office one day a week until the end of August when he will go 3 days a week, although we are manifesting winning the VaxMillions Lottery Giveaway. Ruth Anne's classes are hybrid and she will mask up when she volunteers with ReVision Urban Farm.

While a part of me feels so strongly that if only 'they' would have waited longer to lift all protocols and 'they' would have gotten vaccinated we could have eradicated the virus, I know that my inner world connected to the Divine dictates my quality of life. Suffering is created when we focus on the What if's and If only's pointing fingers creating an us against them kind of world.

We are reinvesting the money we would have used to go to New York City and the theater and Cape Cod into landscaping our house and making home improvements.

———

We are stepping up our gratitude practice reminding ourselves that it is not 2020 but we are not quite out of the pandemic yet....

Soul lessons learned from 2020 will continue to hold us in good stead as we navigate what we hope is the tail end of the pandemic. I will step up my meditation practice, limit exposure to the news, continue to find avenues to share my inspirational message and journey of transformation, and cherish the moments of peace and quiet.

In the Quiet of the Morning

In the quiet of the morning
sunbeams seen through eyes closed
streaming into room
filling me with hope

Cat's purring my soundtrack
connect to Source
sifting and sorting through thousands of thoughts
fleeting moments of doubt and fear

Choosing faith

In mind's eye all is well
trusting Truth from a higher authority
to guide
unleashing imagination

Creation replaces reaction
tears gently trickle
overflow from a grateful heart
beaming blessings to all beings

In the quiet of the morning
joy bubbles from deep within soul
dawn of a new day.

"Imagination is everything. It is the preview of life's coming attractions." ~Albert Einstein

As we set out on our early Monday morning run, I felt a heaviness. I decided I needed to shift out of the state I was in with harnessing the power of the imagination. Massachusetts is offering a VaxMillions lottery for all who have been fully vaccinated in Massachusetts. Today was the second drawing.

"Okay Team," I announced. "Let's practice for when we get the call that we won."

We made sure our phone ringers were on high.

"Hello. May I please speak with Ruth Anne McManus?"

"Yes. This is she."

"This is Mary {pause for a quick second} Rouget from the Department of Public Health. I am calling to congratulate you on winning VaxMillions." I went on to say what the next steps were for her to claim her prize. We burst out laughing with the name I quickly came up with. Ruth Anne took on the persona of Ms. Pickles when she called me.

When it was Tom's turn to win I started crying with gratitude as if he really won. Ruth Anne reminded me that I wasn't supposed to be the one with excitement as the one calling to congratulate him. More laughter as we made our way to the Reservoir.

It was Tom's turn to 'call' me. He put on a foreign accent and we all laughed so hard we could hardly run.

Next we practiced holding the check for our photo. It all felt so real and so wonderful to experience the thrill of receiving a million dollars to be fully vaccinated.

We trusted abundance was on its way and focused on the beauty of a summer's day in Boston where all the troubles of the world just melt away with every foot strike, The sweat poured as the August sun was hot, but there was a delightful cool breeze that kept us comfortable. We talked about the excitement for Tom's upcoming vacation and celebrating the twins' birthday in person a week from Wednesday. We enjoyed a delicious breakfast when we got home and were ready to embrace a new day, a new week and a new month ahead.

Focus

Drowning out the din
focusing on the beauty of a summer morning
I spy with my little eye
magnify the magnificence
through my looking glass

Troubles melt away with sweat
with each foot strike
strength surges
global pandemic still reigns
reigning in my thoughts

focus

Towering trees
a canopy of green
swans swimming
serenity
calming a trembling heart
Divine love triumphs
signs surround

focus.

"When something goes wrong in your life just yell plot twist and move on." *~Anonymous*

On May 29th, all restrictions were lifted in Massachusetts. The vaccine was touted as highly effective. The vaccinated population was told to go forth and resume all their activities. The unvaccinated population were encouraged to get vaccinated and mask up. Cases of COVID-19 plummeted and then "plot twist" - the Delta Variant. As new data emerged, new guidelines for mask wearing and social distancing were put in place to try to contain the sharp uptick in cases.

With an uptick in cases came an uptick of anger and frustration. It seems as though soul lessons that were learned during the pandemic of 'we're all in this together' with kindness and compassion breaking through the once vile diatribe of the previous Presidential administration, is slowly eroding. People expected that with the vaccine, a carefree life would resume just in time for summer.

The pandemic to date has left restaurants short staffed and tempers flaring. It's sad to hear horns honking as soon as the light turns to green. Fear and confusion seem to prevail alongside a sense of bravado in the face of the variant as people attend concerts and go unmasked indoors.

There was an article in the Boston Globe about people lying in an attempt to get a booster shot even though there is no data to support the potential benefit of a booster shot before the end of September.
The anger, fear and panic can be infectious. We noticed that we were getting impatient with our neighbors who have a tendency to walk through our yard and not respect the boundaries of our property. We were going to have a fence installed but then opted for small trees to create a 'natural' boundary. The day came for installation and we were anxious about spending the money with the general uncertainty of the economy, and realized that we needed to be open-hearted and kind even when others were not acting in kind. We were also feeling

anxious about Tom's future at Boston College.

Kurt Vonnegut's quote came to mind: "*Be soft. Do not let the world make you hard. Do not let pain make you hate. Do not let the bitterness steal your sweetness. Take pride that even though the rest of the world may disagree, you still believe it to be a beautiful place.*"

We called the contractor and explained our concerns. He had done our walkway earlier this year and we gave each of his team extra money. We opened our yard to them while they ate their lunch making sure they had what they needed for their big noonday meal. We explained the situation to him and Tom asked him what he wanted for his trouble since he was about to get the trees to plant. He said, "You are my friend. You don't have to pay me a thing. Let me know when you need me." I cried as he spoke from his heart in his thick Brazilian accent.

We had a ladder down in our yard where the trees were going to go to mark the boundary. We took it up. It felt liberating to open our hearts and realize that we ARE all in this together. We are all One.

The divisiveness and rancor from a year ago when the pandemic was raging has returned. We are blessed with strong leaders in President Biden and Vice President Harris. It is up to each and every one of us to do our part to promote kindness and practice compassion especially towards ourselves as we ride the waves of emotions and experiences that the pandemic has left in its wake.

The pandemic 2.0 is definitely a wake-up call for us as a family. We are going to be kind and compassionate with ourselves opening our hearts and trusting the Universe has our back as it always has throughout our lives.

I discovered this meta meditation in my Facebook memory:

May I be happy and have peace of mind
May I be healthy and strong

May I be free of suffering and safe from internal and external harm
May my life be of ease and well-being
May I have a compassionate heart filled with loving kindness
May I be free
May all beings be happy and have peace of mind
May all beings be healthy and strong
May all beings be free of suffering and safe from
 internal and external harm
May all beings have a life of ease and well-being
May all beings have a compassionate heart filled with loving kindness
May all beings be free

As we navigate COVID-19 2.0 may we all dig deep to have patience, compassion and kindness with ourselves and one another.

"Trust the wait. Embrace the uncertainty. Enjoy the beauty of becoming. When nothing is certain, anything is possible." ~Mandy Hale

Uncertainty is a part of life. So often it is a challenge to trust the wait and visualize positive outcomes. Appearances can look dreary and it is easy to get weighed down by current realities. We recently had a very challenging situation at Tom's job. There was ongoing stress due to a number of factors and it finally reached a point where we had to evaluate next steps.

"Change is hardest at the beginning, messiest in the middle and best at the end." ~Anonymous

I've been increasing the time and frequency of my meditation. This morning, this poem flowed through me:

The Present

As I pull the ribbons
unwrapping the gift of a new day
I pause

Will I pass the time with worry and fret
bemoaning the past
erase unhappy thoughts
as easily as wiping a white board clean.

Starting day with clean slate
open heart
deep breaths
grateful
all I need is right here.

In this very moment
creating joy
it's a gift to be alive
challenges transform coal into diamonds.

Twinges of fear
transform What if's
future trusted to the Divine
be present
feel day flowing with ease
graciously greeting
each moment with hope
gift of a new day.

I subscribe to David Hamilton's "Daily Boost." Today's inspiration was: *There are times in life when you just need to let go and take a leap of faith.*

I've been getting signs from songs on the radio and as I released fear and opened myself up to the magic of the Universe, amazing and miraculous things have been happening.

Nothing is ever certain. I believe we have learned that many times over with the pandemic. But we can create certainty in our lives through faith and embracing uncertainty knowing that when nothing is certain, everything is possible.

"You can't stop the waves, but you can learn to surf." ~Jon Kabat Zinn

Several years ago I was blessed to hear Tara Brach speak at the Cambridge Insight Meditation Center. She is a psychologist and meditation teacher who did a Dharma Talk followed by a guided meditation. In the Dharma Talk she shared how one of her students was annoyed because another student was breathing loudly during a meditation. The student thought to themselves that if only the student would stop breathing so loudly, they would be able to meditate better and feel more peace. The other student left the room and do you know what happened? The student realized it didn't make a difference; that the frustration and inability to settle down to experience peace and calm during the meditation was inside of them.

How often do we find ourselves saying these days, "if only." If only my co-worker would leave me alone. If only the pandemic were over. If only it were not raining. You get the idea. The list goes on and on.

Since the diagnosis of Post-Polio Syndrome fourteen years ago and throughout this pandemic, I have become acutely aware that it is up to me to navigate circumstances. I need to take time in the morning for meditation, to make time for meditation in the afternoon and to put on a meditation before sleep. I monitor my state of being throughout the day. Am I in a state of fear or am I in a state of love, connected to Source creating my life rather than reacting to external circumstances. I'll admit, some days it is more challenging to shift from fear to love, but I know for my physical, emotional and spiritual well-being it is imperative that I make that effort to return to a state of love, faith, trust and envisioning what I want to have happen versus dwell in the past or being fearful of the future.

Tom's work has been very challenging with his work place being short staffed while trying to implement innovative technology. We have talked about retirement and set the date for May 25, 2022. My early retirement was on May 25, 2007 and my daughter thought it would make for great symmetry to have him retire on the same day. At the twins birthday party last week, we talked about moving the date way up since Tom was beginning to exhibit some physical symptoms associated with stress. We chose September 20th as the date he will begin the next chapter of his life.

Within a week, while Tom was on vacation, we met so many earth angels and were guided by Spirit to get everything in place to give notice when he returned to work today. I have complete trust and faith in experiencing the flow of abundance even though he will no longer work full time in technology. The synchronicity and serendipity that is already showing itself to us is awe inspiring.

Just as the ocean's waves are forever in a state of ebb and flow, so too are our lives. Of course we all love it when seas are calm and we see for miles to the horizon. But there are times when there may be storms that we have to navigate or fog where we just have to trust even though we can't see very far in front of us. That's the time when faith and trust come rushing in with the tide and we breathe, living only in the eternal present moment.

Navigation

When waves of fear
wash away faith and joy
breathe
feel Divine's presence
coursing through every cell.

When fear tries to pierce heart
allow Divine's Love to be armor
shake off quivering and quaking
let no one put asunder your joy.

Take pause
power pose
claiming birthright
born to be free.

Trip lightly through adversity
eyes on horizon
steady sure footsteps
surging strength from depth of soul.

Lost and confused?

Behold
invisible hand guides safely through storm
follow its lead
to rainbow's end
pot of gold
overflows with well-being.

"The crickets felt it was their duty to warn everybody that summertime cannot last forever. Even on the most beautiful days in the whole year - the days when summer is changing into autumn - the crickets spread the rumor of sadness and change." ~E.B.White

It seems like in the blink of an eye we go from Spring's awakenings with celebrating seeing the first crocus poke through the once frozen ground to the growing crescendo of the cricket's song as hours of daylight diminish.

With all that is happening in the world it would be so easy to get swept up in the "rumor of sadness and change." There is ongoing devastation from the pandemic with the Delta Variant. Fortunately businesses remain open and many events continue to take place.

I received my confirmation from the BAA for my volunteer assignment for packet stuffing.

The BAA is requiring proof of vaccination or a negative COVID-19 test within 48 hours of the assignment. It's an open air warehouse and we could wear masks as an extra layer of protection. But the communication from the BAA notes that they continue to monitor "the situation" and will make decisions based on recommendations from the CDC and public health officials. It continues to feel like a tale of two pandemics. Governor Baker announced today that he is going to require all state workers to be vaccinated; no frequent testing as other localities are doing but vaccination or termination of employment. He has decided to leave mask mandates to localities for now.

There were several concerts at Fenway Park in recent weeks and the Falmouth Road Race took place with 7000 runners finishing the race. Wearing of masks was optional and intermittent. There was a sense of incredible joy that the race returned to a live event. It was the largest race in Massachusetts since March of 2020. Yet in the background, news of increased hospitalizations and rate of infections climbed.

People are trying to balance living life and moving forward as if the pandemic were over. There is ongoing guidance from the Surgeon General, the CDC and local Departments of Public Health. Our Town of Brookline has mandated masks indoors in all municipal buildings. New guidelines have come out for booster shots. It is recommended that people with compromised immune systems receive a booster shot. People are urged to get a booster shot 8 months after being fully vaccinated.

There was such incredible joy and a sense of freedom as we celebrated the sights that heralded Springtime. We expected to experience a summer free from the specter of COVID-19. We thought that having made the choice to be vaccinated would bring with it freedom from masks, a sense of ease and leaving the trauma and stress of the past 18 months in the rear view mirror.

With the cricket's song, I get to choose how to embrace the change in seasons. I leave behind the expectations and disappointment that summer was not as we expected it to be for expectations only create suffering, and turn my attention to all we have to be grateful for. We were able to celebrate the twins' 34th birthday in person. It had been 4 years since our son Autumn and his girlfriend Michelle came to our house. We enjoyed and continue to enjoy evening walks savoring sunsets. We have our health. Tom and Ruth Anne each tested negative for their required COVID-19 tests at Boston College. After a few bumps in the road at work, we are excited for Tom's transition to retirement from full time employment in technology after 40 years. We are blessed with a strong nuclear family that rides through challenges with resilience and a tapestry of care woven with love. We have a fabulous village. Even though we may not see them in person right now, our connections are strong.

The cricket's song will be my soundtrack to dance through the transition from Summer to Autumn accepting what is and being grateful for the many many blessings in our life.

From Crocus to Crickets

Can we eternally experience the hope of seeing the first crocus
even as cricket's song signals summer's demise
can we feel the jubilant joy of springtime even as sun sets earlier each day
seeing buds pregnant with possibilities gives birth to optimism
can Autumn's splendor ignite Spirit's flame?

Can we bend with arc of the seasons
changing landscape of blooms
crescendo of cricket's song
heralding change
embracing transitions
always guided by Light
led by benevolent Beings
seen and unseen
surrounded by Divine Love.

Let melancholy linger for but a moment
remember the caterpillar
be at the ready
transform
soar in midst of uncertainty
a bird's eye view of life
joy in journey
trusting in life's rhythm and flow
all is well and in Divine Order.

Current Situation: Current of Love

"Love is stronger than fear." ~John 1:18

It's time for me once again to only skim the headlines and resist the temptation to click on what's trending on Twitter which usually only takes me down the rabbit hole of news that breeds fear and discontent. I hide posts on Facebook that do not fuel a sense of joy and happiness. I actively seek out people and pages that I know have uplifting messages. I am spending more time reading, meditating and engaging in conversations with family and friends. I am taking more time for walks in addition to my three 5K's a week, and allowing Spirit to flow through me to write.

I ride the waves of fear and anxiety knowing sensations pass and focus on thoughts that can shift me into a state of love, hope, trust, faith and calm. I am mindful of what I am feeding my mind and observe how I respond to situations that are triggers from past trauma. I let healing tears flow when I need to release stress and practice gratitude connecting with Source.

David Hamilton has done extensive research about how kindness is an antidote to stress. Kindness triggers oxytocin, the "feel good hormone" which counters the production of cortisol, the fight/flight hormone. I've joined the #BeKind2021 campaign from the Born This Way Foundation. From September 1st to September 21st, I'll be joining a global community practicing kindness, compassion and gratitude. We'll focus on kindness and compassion for ourselves and others. It's a wonderful way to transform feelings of fear and being separate to becoming aware of what binds us together as a global community. It's a deliberate way to keep thoughts and action in the forefront of our lives that help to counter the stress we are all experiencing at this time.

I'd been waking up at 6am when our beloved cat Jamie woke me up to be fed and I was having trouble getting back to sleep. Often times I would sleep through Jamie's head butts and she would move on to get Tom to feed her. In recent weeks, my vigilant self would get up to feed Jamie enjoying the peace and quiet of the early morning hours. The other morning, I could not settle down observing all the feelings going through me. I opened my heart to Divine Guidance and this poem flowed through me:

Current of Love

Weariness and wariness
hope and immunity waning
sputtering faith
current situation seems dim
transformed
when love lights the way!

Lens of love
prism of possibilities
despite what eye may see
sparks ignite
burn away doubt and despair
Source ever present
at the ready
tune out and tune in
electrify
illuminate
be light
beaming
becoming radiant.

Turn tide of swirling thoughts
what if
worries wash away
what if
happiness and peace prevail
keep the faith
spread the faith
floating on a current of Love conquering fear.

"Nothing is more precious than being in the present moment. Fully alive. Fully aware." ~Thich Nhat Hahn

The forecast was for a possible Category I Hurricane, Henri, heading toward New England. Tom and Ruth Anne said they would stay at home and do storm preparation around the house while I went on a run. While I felt a wee bit guilty leaving them to do the work around the house, they reassured me that they would be fine and I should take advantage of the solitude of my run.

The weather was hot and humid. I had to slow down my pace and take notice of the spectacular scenes created by the Master Artist's Hand as I ran around the Reservoir. It was an incredible gift to have time to just be. As sweat poured, I surrendered to the heat of the day while witnessing the incredible cloud formations and the colors of a late August sky. Ruth Anne and Tom had almost finished getting the "perimeter secured" when I returned home. We sat down together and had a cool refreshing glass of sparkling water. I expressed my heartfelt gratitude for my time of solitude with Source.

Saturday's run inspired this poem:

Expansion

Running under canopy of white puffy clouds
gaze grazes to August's azure sky
perfect painting reflected on still water
does mind wander to prediction of impending storm
surrender to savor peaceful present
a gift from Master Artist's heart.
Heart opens
sweat pours from every pore
cleansing heart and soul
wringing out worry and fear
in its wake peace
joy to be alive reflecting on gratitude.

Contrast to contraction
expanding thoughts with every breath
step by step
moving with grace and ease
trust and faith
tethered to Source
as cloudy thoughts clear
revealing the Masterpiece of my life.

May we all find a path to feeling our hearts expand and time to just be.

P.S Hurricane Henri brought a little wind and a little rain to New England. I was reminded of Mark Twain's quote, *"I've had a lot of worries in my life, most of which never happened."*

"Outer order contributes to inner calm." ~Gretchen Rubin

When the pandemic first began, we did a LOT of decluttering. We rearranged furniture and created space as we entered a time of needing to spend the majority of our time at home. After the Boston Marathon bombings, we did a massive decluttering of our home and had a company haul away what was once stashed in our dormer, basement and closets that we no longer needed. If anything were to happen to my husband and me, we did not want our adult children left with sorting through what we collected through decades of being together.

This summer has been one of the 6th hottest on record in Boston. We endured our fourth heat wave this past week. While I am deeply grateful to air conditioning, I have a love/hate relationship with it. I don't sleep as well when the windows are closed with the a/c on. I feel confined when it's unhealthy to be outdoors and the heat index is over 100 degrees. After several days of heat advisories, I needed to do something to elevate my mood. Options were a bit limited again as cases of COVID-19 with the variant are on the rise and there is a new indoor mask mandate. While we continued to go on our runs, we had to limit time outside due to the heat advisory.

It was time to look around the house and create outer order to feed my inner calm that was waning with the news of booster shots, mask mandates and continued division in our country. People tend to forget that there is more to unite us than there is to divide us. I am blessed that my Facebook newsfeed is filled with quotes from light workers and I stay closely connected with those who express love and light in their quotes. I continue to resist the temptation to go to CNN.com or click on what's trending on Twitter that will invariably take me down the rabbit hole of negativity.

Ruth Anne and I cleaned out clothes in her closet. What a delicious feeling to donate clothes that were reminders of a time when she was wasn't well. We sorted through the linen closet, and the kitchen.

Tom and I decided to rearrange the home office. On September 17th, he bids his 6 1/2 year technology career at Boston College farewell. He is eligible for retirement at almost 70 years old and we had planned for retirement next Spring. But sometimes the Universe has other plans. We decided to take a collective leap of faith. To calm the butterflies, we created outer order with a cleaner look to our space in the office and living room. Tom was able to create inner space by doing exit interviews with upper management explaining why he was leaving. It was liberating for him to share why he needed to leave and the toll the job was taking on his health and life/work balance.

Classes start on Tuesday for Ruth Anne and will be hybrid meeting in person and on line. We are excited that she will be able to be on campus where everyone must be vaccinated. While there is an air of excitement, we could anticipate this transition with greater joy if the pandemic were completely behind us. But we move forward celebrating health and well-being, the gift of the vaccine and trust that soon the pandemic will be a distant memory. Her room is arranged and ready for a successful semester of studies and working part-time. As she was anticipating her schedule for the semester, she briefly became anxious and overwhelmed. She realized that something had to go as her schedule was too cluttered. While she dearly loves ReVision Urban Farm and planned to volunteer every other week at their stand at the Farmer's Market, she realized it would not afford her the opportunity to get her Saturday run on and be available for group projects as the semester gathered momentum.

We composed an email to the staff at the Farm and breathed a collective sigh of relief that we decluttered our Saturday schedule.

What a productive day of decluttering in many ways and on many levels for Team McManus! It felt so good to take a deep breath and prepare to enter a new season with open space on the calendar, in our physical space in the house and in our inner space. We spent time together, unplugged processing how we are coping with the ongoing pandemic and discovering what we need to thrive and have a sense of well-being during these turbulent times.

———

Every month I change up my twice weekly strength training routine. As I turned the page in my journal, I looked through its pages. I tore off the pages that held energy from the past and created space to energize a future of abundance, health and well-being. I decluttered my email and updated social media photos.

As the heat wave broke in the evening, we opened the windows and turned off the air conditioners. In the stillness of evening we sat and listened to the crickets who loudly sang their song. They were inviting us to embrace the season of change, transitions and letting go of what we no longer need in our lives.

Embracing Change

As leaves' vibrant green begins to fade
cricket's song grows louder
as sun sets earlier every day
change is on the horizon.

Autumn's splendor on its way
nature's ebb and flow
juxtaposition of beauty and loss
heralding a new season.

Surrender to seasons of life
Divine Love surrounding
Tempo tempers fear of a trembling heart
heartful of faith.

Tempest of emotions
quieted in stillness
serenaded by sounds of silence
ready to embrace change.

"Always live in the higher vibrational frequencies of love, gratitude and possibility." ~Anonymous

There are times when I feel my energy wane and my mood shift to feeling edgy and 'down.' I limit my intake of news but do need to keep informed about the latest guidance from the CDC and local public health officials. In our little corner of the world, there are major changes happening with Tom's job and Ruth Anne's miraculous ongoing healing journey. While at times I feel incredibly hopeful and optimistic about these changes, at times my 'Negative Nancy' mindset takes over. Tears of gratitude that I know all is well and in Divine Order mix with an unsettling sense of fear. I focus my imagination on what I DO want rather than focus on negative outcomes.

When we were waiting for the results of Tom and Ruth Anne's COVID-19 tests last year, Ruth Anne came up with a song called, "Raise Your Vibration". She repeated raise your vibration several times and followed it with "You gotta plump plump plump your cells." It's a song we returned to this year while waiting for test results and one we often turn to raise our vibration.

During these times, it can be challenging to always live in the higher vibrational frequencies. When I feel myself slipping into fear and worry, I nudge myself back to the gift of the present. Rather than harping on untoward outer appearances, I settle into dwelling in the present moment seeking out all that is right and good in my life. Sometimes I walk around my home giving thanks for the 'little things' like rolls of toilet paper, a refrigerator full of food, running water, air conditioning and a spacious home that is filled with love from my husband, daughter and our beautiful cat Jamie.

After dinner last night, we were feeling tired but knew how wonderful it would be to take a walk around the neighborhood. We breathed deeply letting go of any worry or fret. As our walk progressed, we were treated to the most incredible sunset. A feast for our eyes was accompanied by the sounds of the crickets' songs. How could we possibly worry about anything when we bear witness to this expansive sky with incredible majesty reminding us of something far greater at work in the Universe.

I received a letter from Social Security telling me that I was denied for Medicare Part B. Part of Tom's separation from Boston College has involved getting health care. I marvel at how the Universe led me to just right the person when I first looked at Medicare options. We were waiting for the Medicare Part B to be put in place so we could sign up for a Medicare Advantage Plan. I was just about to pick up the phone to call Social Security prepared for at least a 30 minute wait, when the phone rang. It was the health insurance agent I had contacted who called to inform me that I'd been approved for Medicare Part B and we could sign up for the additional coverage. I told him what happened and expressed deep heartfelt gratitude for him for his diligent follow up. Today, Tom received his new Medicare card and signed up for his supplemental coverage. We are healthy and don't often use our health insurance, but like car insurance, it is a comfort to know it's there should we need it.

When I believe and see that everything is falling into place, worries melt away. I get out of the way and allow the Universe to work its magic.

If I am stuck in the mire of worry, I am not open to those delicious feelings of love, gratitude and possibility.

In the midst of uncertainty and times when the headlines can make the hair on the back of your neck stand on end, it's the very time to raise your vibration!

Raise Your Vibration

Fear and worry can shake us to the core
flashbacks to trauma and all that went before
headlines about tragedy leave us bereft of hope
take deep breaths letting go to forge a path to better cope.

Have trust to believe what eye does not yet see
Source's well of Love bathes all Beings to be free
light and ease and grace raining down cup your hand
plant your feet unwavering in faith we take our stand.

Live as if the dreams you dream so deep within your heart
are playing out right here and now no waiting for their start
purposes and passions unveil Truth let beauty shine
abundance, joy and happiness inheritance now is thine.

Raise your vibration sing out clear and sing out strong
Divinity's proximity is right where we belong
safe harbor from tumultuous times trembling heart now steady beat
as a new day now is dawning open door to future greet.

"Be kind whenever possible. It's always possible." ~The 14th Dalai Lama

I think of the Born This Way #BeKind21 campaign as a mirror reminding me to be aware of the choices I make with thoughts and behaviors as I go about my day. I realize how easy it is to judge someone if I am not mindful of my thoughts and what is in my heart. These past few days have been a wonderful opportunity to put kindness and compassion front and center. I have the tab to the #BeKind21 campaign open on my computer and it's a nudge from the Universe to choose kindness and compassion for myself and others. On Wednesday we greeted parents and children on their way to school with warm smiles wishing them well on their first day of school. Yesterday I focused on gratitude.

While it's always possible to be kind, it's not always easy.

We've encountered some challenging situations in recent weeks. The encounters reached a head and tempers flared. I suggested to Tom that we take the 'high road' and apologize even though the other person demonstrated unkind and cruel behaviors.

With all that is happening in the world, the #BeKind21 campaign is Divine Timing. David Hamilton, my good friend and the "kindness czar" for Psychologies Magazine on Facebook shared this post about the #BeKind21 campaign. Several years ago he went to New York to be a part of Born This Way Foundation's kindness campaign with Lady Gaga. David lives in Scotland.

Today (1st September) marks the beginning of #bekind21

The aim is to do an act of kindness (or more) a day each day through until 21st September.

As I wrote in an earlier post, last year, there were over 100 million acts of kindness!! I think we can surpass 200 million this year. This is how we can make a difference in the world. Collectively. With our hearts.

It's been my personal observation that kindness rescues us sometimes. There are times when it's just what you need - either the thing itself or even just the knowing that someone cares in that moment.

And as the giver, I feel that kindness accesses that part deep within us that just knows that kindness, compassion, empathy, an act of love, is the right thing to do. I suppose, in these moments we rescue ourselves. We gain perspective on what really matters out of the multitude of competing interests that fill our minds each and every day.

I've joined the #bekind21 campaign this year. You can register here: https://bornthisway.foundation/bekind21/

There's also a cool kindness calendar on the registration page that you can download to keep track of your kindnesses. I have mine on my wall.

Wherever you are, I wish you a great day. And remember to be kind. It's almost always the right thing to do.

I've been working on this poem that I was able to finish after yesterday's afternoon meditation:

Choose Kind

When heart is hurt it may be difficult to find
a path to healing to be gracious be kind
remember a bully has wounds that run deep
invisible to eye hidden secrets they keep.
A burden they carry defensive and cruel
retaliation revenge only serves anger to fuel

don't turn a blind eye see beyond behavior so hurtful and cold
a daring perception be brave and be bold.
A gift of choosing love to thine own self be true
reconciliation remember they're a person too
don't let the wound fester let go let in light
your Spirit will thank you peace well within sight.
Underneath all the layers of bitterness bluster
beats a heart that's Divine if only courage they could muster
with compassion forgiveness choosing tender thoughts I'll be free
kind-hearted and vulnerable I'll let myself be.

I am often asked in interviews how I stayed connected to my
goodness, and live my life as a kind and compassionate Being
despite all the trauma I endured as a child after contracting paralytic
polio. I drew from a touch of grace that I experienced after
contracting paralytic polio feeling pure Divine Love after an out of
body experience. I share how, after the diagnosis of Post-Polio
Syndrome, I realized that I needed to transform and heal the anger
and hurts through the power of forgiveness. I saw all that happened
to me through the lens of gratitude. I embraced my experiences as
gifts and once I opened my heart to love myself and forgive those
who hurt me, I began to heal mind, body and soul.

I am inspired by the #BeKind21 campaign and the messages that the
Born This Way Foundation is sharing in daily emails.

Let us all create a vibration of kindness and care throughout every
day of every month.

*"The world has been heavy. Let's lift each other up." ~Born This
Way Foundation*

"Running has the power to heal.
Running unites.
Running creates community.
Running nourishes the soul.
Run for lifelong friendships.
Run for health.
Run for happiness.
Running clears the mind.
Running strengthens the body.
Running is hard work.
Hard work is rewarding.
Running should be enjoyed.
Relish every step. xoxo Shalane"

I have been relishing every step of my runs this week. Shalane Flanagan's quote sums up the power and joy of running. It has been a Godsend throughout the pandemic. While I always celebrate the gift of running in my life, this week running has been a sanctuary and a time to process and debrief from all that happened at Tom's work this past year that led to our leap of faith decision. There's been a lot of stress during the transition especially from two of the managers, and it's been a major trauma trigger for me. I also experienced the trigger of my dad's suicide 50 years ago when we ended up needing to declare bankruptcy after his death.

Through meditation and staying connected to Source, heeding the messages I was receiving through songs on the radio, friends' Facebook posts and conversations with friends and family, I pried my body out of the past and into experiencing the delicious gift of precious moments. Tom is almost 70 years old and I will be 68 on Christmas Day. We will be married 44 years next year. While we both want to live and enjoy being in our physical bodies for years to come, we are keenly aware how tomorrow is never promised as we've seen during the pandemic. As I've shifted my energy, I've started seeing a shift in the news I am receiving. Immunity is not waning as originally thought. There is a halt on rushing out to get a booster shot as the vaccine proves to be highly effective. Vaccination rates are on the rise and while masks are needed right now, there is much hope that the pandemic will become something that we live with such as colds or the flu.

Today was a glorious end of summer day. A vibrant blue sky with white puffy clouds, warm sunshine and low humidity made for perfect weather for our Saturday morning run. Even though Tom is on his last on call weekend for work, we went to South Boston for our run. My soul was craving to be near the ocean. Right before we were about to leave we were inspired to pack a picnic, beach chairs and towels just in case we wanted to put our toes in the water after our run.

We had a splendid run.

Because of the pandemic, they removed porta-potties along the route. I suggested we wait to use the bathrooms at the beach or go in the ocean but there was no time to waste. Apparently this happened to Tom while out on long runs and he knew how to get into the health club at a nearby apartment complex. I waited outside trusting I could wait until I got back to the beach. Tom said that we were residents and the security gentleman let them use the rest rooms. Just as we were about to finish the run Tom asked, "Where's my phone?" He had to run back to get it. I prayed the entire time that it was still in the restroom and no one would ask him about what unit he lived in or his name.

After I went to the bathroom and Ruth Anne and I were unloading our picnic, I received a text. Tom took a selfie and he looked incredibly satisfied with the successful outcome of his mission. The sun was hot but there was a comfortable breeze to keep us cool. We would have been fine to sit on the beach, but the water and waves called to us. Ruth Anne and I love to swim. With the pandemic we have avoided gyms like well, the plague. We didn't have our bathing suits. That has never stopped us before from going into the ocean after a run. Fortunately it was high tide. We didn't have to walk far to get into water where we could swim. Ruth Anne dove in before me and she encouraged me with a 1-2-3 go. It was a baptism into the new phase of life we are entering with Tom's retirement from full time technology work and Ruth Anne returning to part-time work and graduate school. I have more time to focus on writing and healing.

After playing in the water together, we dried off in the sun before heading home.

Today was one of those perfect 10 days that was a reflection of a lot of inner work I have been doing this past month. Meditation, faith, clearing out old thought patterns and beliefs culminated in a day overflowing with joy, health and well-being. My heart overflowed with infinite gratitude for the gift of being alive with all of life's blessings. With love, gratitude, faith and shifting attention away from fear and old beliefs, we can heal and overcome creating infinite possibilities in our lives.

"Worry is a prayer for chaos." ~Gabby Bernstein

I've been riding the waves that go with a big life change of Tom's retirement. While I limit my exposure to news, the "dreadlines" seemed to have had a bigger impact on me in recent days. I found myself getting stuck in a cycle of worry and fear. I know that worrying is praying for something we do not want to have happen and that it is vital to look within to create my outer world. I believe we are all feeling a little weary of the ongoing pandemic, extreme weather and fires, and a "shaky" economic outlook.

After being in my head for a bit during yesterday's 5K run, I shared with Tom and Ruth Anne what was weighing me down. I was stuck on the falsehoods that they threw at Tom during the "Performance Improvement" meeting and was concerned they would dock his pay as was insinuated in an email. With the vast ocean on my right and loving daughter and husband by my side, I was able to purge myself of the fear and worry. I ended up doing major negative splits on our 5K dripping with sweat and a little dizzy from my effort. Cold water, a banana and a picnic lunch was the quick remedy to help me recover.

My favorite quote from Ruth Anne was, "Mom...how can you let these dreary thoughts be on such a perfect day?"

She was right!

We played in the water and "practiced" our synchronized swimming feeling the joy of just being in the moment.

As we sat in the sun drying off from our swim, this poem flowed through me:

Baptism

Feet glide along silky silt ocean's floor
wading into gentle waves
expanding
fathom infinite gratitude and love
warm sun on skin
seagulls song entreating.

Dive into faith
releasing fears
fully present
prepared to receive gift of new life
past washed away in tide
only good tidings.

Source's presence palpable
as joy rises from depths of soul
return to innocence
carefree
just Be
believe!

Seize the moment
seas current comforts
get carried away
on this end of summer day
delicious delight
as heart takes flight.

A run, a swim, lots of sun and connecting to Source were the perfect combination to help me release fear and worry and embrace infinite possibilities for a new chapter in our life.

I heard Tom get up several times last night. I reminded myself all is well and in Divine Order. He couldn't sleep and was inspired to go on a technical recruiting website and set his resume status to contract work. In the morning, he told me that he feels he still has a lot of life left in him to do contract work in technology. Within minutes three contract remote jobs popped up that he applied for.

I was about to ask "Are there a lot of remote contract jobs available?" when I heard Spirit say in a British accent, "Are there a lot of remote contract jobs?" I tried to place whose voice was speaking and what movie it was from. It finally clicked. It was Emily Blunt from "Mary Poppins" in the song 'Trip a Little Light Fantastic." The children ask if Mary Poppins can speak 'leary', the language of the lamp lighters and she replies with, "Can I speak leary?" Lin-Manuel Miranda's character says, "Of course she can. She's Mary Poppins!"

During this morning's meditation, I was able to discern the origin of my intense reaction to Tom's manager. I remembered how being unfairly blamed by my alcoholic father was a life and death situation. Tom's job is not life or death unless he were to stay there enduring the untenable stress that could have caused major health problems. It's a job and the Universe has infinite sources of abundance.

This morning I put on "Trip a Little Light Fantastic" and several other uplifting songs from the movie soundtrack while I did my strength training work out. We all have the magic of Mary Poppins within us and whenever worry, doubt or fear rears its head, I will trip a little light fantastic and be ever so grateful for all that is and all that is yet to arrive in our lives.

#BeKind21 A Trip to the Post Office – Kindness is Contagious
September 8, 2021

I had my pants and return label ready to go to the Post Office for two days. I took them to the car as being one step closer to actually getting them to the Post Office. After I dropped my daughter off for her acupuncture appointment this morning, Spirit nudged me to go to a Post Office that I usually don't go to but that was close to her acupuncturist.

"Stand back there and wait for me to call you," the Postal Service worker barked at the man in front of me. "And make sure you are standing apart behind the blue lines. That's what they are there for."

A man with a passport application angrily walked away from the window mumbling something about filing a lawsuit.

While I wanted to leave and go to the Post Office I usually go to, I felt the need to stay there.

"You wait there. She was ahead of you."

The gentleman in front of me said he was going to use the automatic machine but quickly returned saying it was out of order. I struck up a conversation with him about how COVID-19 2.0 seems to be leaving everyone feeling irritable. We chatted a bit about vaccines and masks before I shifted the conversation to gratitude. We smiled with our eyes and agreed that while things might seem worse, at some point the tide will turn and it will get better.

As he took his turn at the counter, a short in stature Asian woman came up right behind me in line with her mask beneath her nose. I warmly greeted her in response to her comment that there was not a long line today and asked her to please step behind the blue line for social distancing as the man behind the counter was enforcing the rules today.

"Oh yes yes," she said. "You are absolutely right."

She quickly adjusted her face mask.

The gentleman who had been in front of me turned as he went to leave wishing me a good day.

"Can I help you?" the Postal Service worker asked.

"Oh yes," I said. "I need a lot of help."

"Are you mailing these pants? This box is way too big."

"I'm sorry," I said. "That's why I didn't package it up. I have a prepaid label and a packing slip....You know I would like to just really thank you for your service. I know it's not easy working for the government under the best of circumstances. I worked at the VA for almost 20 years. I can only imagine the challenges you face every day during COVID-19."

"Thank you. Just for that I am going to get this all packaged up for you and not even charge you for the envelope."

"I'm so grateful to you for helping me."

"There's a lot to be grateful for right now...like this weather. I walk to work every day."

While he took care of everything for my package, we chatted for a few more minutes and said goodbye.

As I left, I whispered to my new friend in the line behind me, "Be sure to thank him."

I started walking down the ramp to exit the Post Office and out of the corner of my eye I saw her walk up to the window. She put her whole body and being into saying, "You extraordinary!" I heard him say "Thank you!" and I smiled knowing that the ripples from those Post Office encounters would create a wonderful vibration in my Town and beyond.

David Hamilton has done extensive research and writing on the benefits of kindness including how it is contagious. His blog, 'How Kindness is Contagious' is as timely today as it was ten years ago when he wrote it. Last March, David wrote in his blog, "*The Most Contagious Thing is Kindness, So while we increase our physical distance to help reduce the likelihood of contagion of coronavirus, let us increase the contagion of kindness instead.*"

As evidenced by my recent trip to the Post Office, there is an urgent need to increase the contagion of kindness. It all begins with one person. May you be 'patient zero.'

"The more you are in a state of gratitude, the more you will attract things to be grateful for." ~Walt Disney

In the midst of challenging times, when anxiety overtakes the mind and body, it can be difficult to shift the focus to gratitude. And yet that is just the time we need to focus on gratitude. When I look back over the past several years, it is easy to feel anger and outrage at how my daughter's condition was misdiagnosed, and mistreated but instead, I focus on the earth angels who finally came into our lives to help Ruth Anne to heal.

As I waited for Ruth Anne at Spaulding Rehab while she had her appointment with Erin, her earth angel Occupational Therapist, my heart opened with gratitude for her healing and recovery.

As I saw the plexiglass partitions on the Constitution Cafe's tables, the signs about Infection Control, the need for all staff to be vaccinated by October 15th, the therapeutic pool devoid of aquatics classes and the empty gift shop, I felt the sadness and grief that hung in the silence. The Front Desk Ambassador, Margaret, who we have known from when I took aquatics at Spaulding and then going to appointments with Ruth Anne told us that they were hoping to open the pool in September but now, "Who knows?"

There's hand sanitizer and masks when you first enter the building and there is no more public access to the cafeteria or the pool. The hustle and bustle of staff gathering in the cafeteria, patients and family members moving out and about the first floor and garden area and the sense of Spaulding's community is noticeably absent. It's so easy to focus on all that is missing in our lives right now, especially after our sense of freedom and ease in the early days post-vaccination. But focusing on what's missing drains me of my energy and tends to turn on the biochemistry of negative "What if's."

I sat down in the lobby of the hospital since it was raining outside, took a few deep, cleansing breaths and this poem flowed out of me:

Magic of Gratitude

Like a magic wand
gratitude whisks away all fear
conjuring a delicious recipe for life
open heart
bubbling over with joy
salty tears trickle
eyes feasting on simple pleasures
sunrises and sunsets
lingering luscious scent of summer
rippling of waves an aural delight
sun's warmth from Source kisses skin
a taste of heaven

Grateful for precious gift of life
Love greater than fear
sprinkle sparkling eyes everywhere I go
reflecting blessings
kindle kindness and compassion
pass the torch of thankfulness
spread seeds of hope
let the magic begin!

"Gratitude turns what we have into enough, and more. It turns denial into acceptance, chaos into order, confusion into clarity...it makes sense of our past, brings peace for today, and creates a vision for tomorrow." ~Melody Beattie

"That happens in life sometimes, doesn't it? Something terrible happens and you think it's the worst thing ever and then it turns out to be the best." ~Sarah Morgan

As my head swirled with negative thoughts of "What if's" I told myself to stop and shift the "What if's" to positive outcomes. On August 5, Tom was given a Performance Improvement Plan at work. He had been working day and night after having had an adverse reaction to the COVID-19 vaccine. He planned to get the vaccine on his vacation but they told him he had to postpone his vacation. He couldn't postpone his 2nd shot and worked when he should have taken time to rest. He was also called back early from his vacation to work the evening before he was to return to work.

He made errors that were uncharacteristic for him and exaggerated by others because of the extraordinary stress everyone experienced. Management didn't check in with him to see what was going on. Instead they "wrote him up" and gave him a warning that if he did not follow the PIP and immediately improve, he would be fired!

Fortunately his vacation started the next week. As Divine Timing would have it, our son Autumn and his partner Michelle were coming to town on August 11th to celebrate the twins' birthday. Team McManus had a meeting and unanimously decided it was time for Tom to retire. We had savings and were totally confident that he could get a low key job somewhere to supplement retirement and social security. The "Big Quit" can be as infectious as COVID-19 and we decided that life is too short to suffer in a work environment. Autumn and Tom got very excited about a dream they've had for several years to have their own technology consulting company.

Last week, there was a meeting scheduled with a top manager on his calendar. "What if they are going to ask you to stay?" {Note how this was quite a shift from what if they tell you to leave early without pay?} "I'm not going to do it," Tom said. We ignored the 'dreadlines' about an uncertain economy trusting that the technology sector is in dire need of talent.

I thought of the Helen Keller quote about security, *"Security is mostly a superstition. It does not exist in nature, nor do the children of men as a whole experience it. Avoiding danger is no safer in the long run than outright exposure."*

The meeting was rescheduled and then canceled. He received a call at 8:30am on Friday morning informing him that his access had been terminated. We were very confused and tried to discern what he was being told. Because he had a high security clearance, they could not let him finish out his last week. The manager reassured us that as far as HR was concerned, nothing about his September 17th end date had changed.

My heart raced for a bit until we were able to process that this was standard operating procedure and had been done with another employee when he left several months ago. He would get his pay for the week but did not have to work! Wow! It felt like the total grace for all the extra hours he worked and stress he endured. It was a bit unsettling that he no longer had access to his email but texts from his co-workers let him know what they had been told by management; that Tom was leaving on good terms and they had to do this for the sake of computer security.

I am in awe of how we mobilized since we made the decision that it was time for Tom to retire from his current position and the magic of the Universe creating miracles at every turn. Health insurance, dental insurance and a new laptop came together with ease. Once he posted his resume, his phone rang off the hook. We prepared both a tech and a non-tech resume. We thought he would do contract work if he stayed in technology or get a job where he could use his incredible interpersonal, customer service and administrative skills.

Plot twist! He has one job offer and is close to getting another offer. He planned on taking the first offer when he had a 2nd interview for a job at another company. He wasn't going to take the interview but it was with a former co-worker from years ago and he was planning to just catch up. The Universe is full of surprises. It was as though no time had passed and the person with whom he interviewed who would be his co-worker said that he would LOVE to work with Tom again. They are expediting the interview process and Tom will have his choice of where he wants to work. Even though he is almost 70 years old, he loves technology, innovation and being part of a collaborative team. Unfortunately, he got burned out and temporarily lost his passion.

What we thought was the worst thing that could have happened to an almost 70 year old man transformed into the best thing that could have happened for spiritual growth for all of us as well as feeling the power of being able to stand up for what is right and true.

We knew it was time for Tom to leave his old job given the physical symptoms he was experiencing from the stress and the reaction to the vaccine but we thought he could just 'hang in there' for several more months while retirement continued to build and COVID-19 subsided. We couldn't have imagined that he would secure another job with benefits for however long he wants to work and to be able to work remote even after the pandemic is under better control.

His health issues have all resolved and the severe back pain he experienced has healed. He feels more vibrant and better than he has in a few years.

We rode a lot of wild waves of emotions these past several weeks intensified by the continued rise in COVID-19 cases. There is continued divisiveness around vaccines and mask mandates. I harness the power of my faith holding a vision of health, healing and well-being for my family, my community, my country and the global community that it's gonna be alright!

"Don't use your energy to worry. Use your energy to believe, create trust, grow and heal." ~Heal Documentary

It's All Right

It's all right to be afraid
surrender to uncertainty
I am here
It's all right to be unsure
feeling unsteady
butterfly quakes before it flies
free from cocoon's confinement
It's all right to shed tears
letting go of how it hurt
I bless and kiss your wounds
It's all right to feel the heal
past is passed
let me light the way
It's all right to trust
feel faith bathe cells
eradicating all that went before
It's all right to set your gaze on goodness
hope on horizon
joyful heart as gratitude flows
It's all right
dream
believing is seeing beyond appearances
see your heart's desire live happily
It's all right to smile
knowing
all here now
is all right.

End of Summer Treat Under the Crescent Moon

"Perhaps the crescent moon smiles in doubt at being told that it is a fragment awaiting perfection." *~Rabindranath Tagore*

I was inspired to write a poem about the crescent moon even though the moon was in a different phase at the time I wrote it:

Crescent Moon

A beacon of hope
smiling as I gaze upon crescent moon
out of plain sight
its powerful presence
seen in mind's eye

Imagination lights the way
wholeness
transforming
transcending
phasing out fear and doubt
seeing beyond appearances

Much lies beyond this silver sliver in the sky
orb of infinite possibilities
all unveiled in Divine Timing
enjoying glow of anticipation
when all is revealed once more!

I was captivated by its image in my mind's eye and what it represents.

Imagine my surprise when we went out for an end of summer treat at Cabot's, an iconic ice cream place we had not been to in years, and there was the crescent moon.

Before the pandemic, we would not take photos in front of Cabot's. Yet these simple pleasures take on a much deeper meaning as the mundane becomes extraordinary. We celebrated how Cabot's made it through the pandemic and was continuing to thrive albeit with masks for employees and diners when they weren't eating or drinking. There was an awareness of social distancing and contactless payment. They used to be a cash only operation.

On May 29th, we celebrated the end of a State of Emergency here in Massachusetts and, as a fully vaccinated family, what we thought would be the end of mask mandates and social distancing. We have learned that, despite all that is going on with the pandemic, or perhaps because of all that is going on with the pandemic, we savor the taste of an end of summer treat with more gusto feeling connected to something far greater than ourselves under the crescent moon.

"The moon is a loyal companion. It never leaves. It's always there watching, steadfast, knowing us knowing us in our light and dark moments, changing forever just as we do. Every day it's a different version of itself. Sometimes weak and wan, sometimes strong and full of light. The moon understands what it means to be human. Uncertain. Alone. Cratered by imperfections. " ~Tahereh Mafi

Three weeks from today, 20,000 runners will toe the starting line of the 125th Boston Marathon while thousands of other runners around the globe will be running a virtual race. The light of the rising moon symbolized emerging from the tight grip the pandemic had on Boston and the world for the past 18 months.

When we considered where to run on Saturday, I felt a profound pull to the Newton Hills. I smile as I write this remembering last year when we decided we were so over the Boston Marathon and running on Heartbreak Hill. Once you have run the Boston Marathon, it becomes a part of the very fiber of your being and keeps calling you back to be a part of its energy. Our running Club, L Street Running Club, was planning to do their last long run from Cleveland Circle to Wellesley College. We were hoping to see some of our beloved Club members who we haven't seen in a year and a half.

While the marathon will be very different this year without Athlete's Village and runners starting their marathon as soon as they arrive in Hopkinton, the need for vaccination or negative COVID-19 test, no kissing the girls in Wellesley or taking food from spectators along the course, and an Expo that will be without the Runners Speakers Series, the Spirit of the Marathon is powerful beyond words this year.

Charity runners were out in full force. What a thrill to see Charity Teams' water stops and familiar faces from our running village. We didn't see anyone from L Street but did see a number of people we've known through the years. We walked a bit with a woman who was struggling on the Hills; not an uncommon occurrence during the last long training run for Boston.

"Is this your first Boston?"

"Yes I came up from New York."

"What charity team are you running with?"

———

When she mentioned the name I commented, "Oh that's who my friend Amanda is running with."

"Yes I know her. She's been great helping me get ready."

"Well let me tell you my story that you can take with you to finish this run and to have with you on Marathon Monday."

I went on to share my journey on the road to the 2009 Boston Marathon. She thanked me as she went on her way.

After sharing my Facebook post about our run, we reconnected with even more runners from our village. Amanda shared how her friend had met me and was inspired by my story when they gathered after the long run. It's a very odd time of year to be experiencing the thrill of the countdown to the Boston Marathon but everything has been odd during these past 18 months. On October 3rd, we are going to do packet stuffing with masks, gloves, proof of vaccination, social distancing and air hugs. The last time we did packet stuffing was after the 2013 bombings. It seems appropriate to be doing this as we emerge (we hope) from the pandemic.

I had one of my best times for a 5K in a very long time on Saturday's run. The hill from the Johnny Kelley Statue is typically an arduous climb for me but the infectious energy from the other runners seemed to sweep me along.

Although gentle high fives in passing replaced usual sweaty hugs and shout outs replaced stopping to chat, there was that familiar feeling with all of the pageantry and festivities that always accompanies the last long run before Boston runs again. Halloween replaced Easter as the holiday to celebrate. It was an extraordinary time on Heartbreak Hill that marked the last long run before we countdown to an iconic live event that signifies we are slowly emerging from the pandemic.

Being Found

The light of the almost full moon drew me into its spell
spellbound
caught by surprise to see it rising in the evening sky
a canopy of leaves framed magnificent marvel.

I was inspired to dance
tripping the light fantastic
as I once had as a lithe ballerina
moments of being fully present
bathed in moonbeams
past whisked away.

Awe and wonder
wandering no more
eternal and ethereal
pondering magical magnificence
I am found!

"Life starts all over again when it gets crisp in the fall." *~F. Scott Fitzgerald*

The end of summer often triggers a sense of sadness. It's often difficult to experience a sense of rebirth and renewal when the leaves are changing colors and falling to the ground and yet Autumn can be a time of incredible transformation and new beginnings as we let go of what no longer serves us opening our hearts to the infinite possibilities not yet visible to the eyes.

One week ago, Tom left his job as a full time employee with benefits. We created our own benefit package now that we are both over 65 and tightly held hands as we took this leap of faith. It's the second leap of faith we took together. We took one for me 15 years ago after I was diagnosed with Post-Polio Syndrome. While a leap of faith can be frightening, there is a feeling of exhilaration and excitement with what is on the horizon. Sometimes I get caught in the vortex of fear spiraling downward in my thoughts and energy. But then I take a look back at all that I have created in my life during these past 15 years, and see the signs surrounding now that all is well and in Divine order.

Tom and I have been on a journey of letting go, discernment and experiencing the excitement that a new season brings in our lives. I had a few brief moments of solar plexus clutching fear about finances which was a flashback to experiences from my youth. Once I released the fear, the magic of the Universe is swirling around us just like the colorful autumn leaves that will soon be dancing in the cool, crisp air. There are events happening in Autumn this year that usually happen in Spring and Summer. The world still seems topsy turvy as we find ways to live with COVID-19.

The Boston Marathon traditionally takes place in April as Spring begins to bloom in Boston. There are blossoms on the trees that line Commonwealth Avenue and winter's chill begins to yield to warmer days with more hours of daylight. This year, the Marathon takes place on October 11th which is also Indigenous Peoples Day. Foliage should be at its peak with many trees already showing bare branches. Instead of homes along the route being decorated for Easter and Spring festivities, Halloween decorations, pumpkins and mums will be the decor of the day.

The Tony Awards typically take place in the summer but this year were postponed until this Sunday because of COVID-19. Rather than warm gentle breezes welcoming nominees on the Red Carpet, there will be a bit of a chill in the air. Broadway is slowly reopening in New York but mask wearing and vaccinations are mandated for audiences at least through November 1st. I don't believe there will be a Red Carpet. After Tony parties have been cancelled. But just like the Spirit of the Marathon rises from the ashes of the pandemic, the lights of Broadway shine on with hearts overflowing with gratitude that iconic institutions and events live on.

This is the first year that I can remember when I have not felt sadness about summer coming to an end. I focused on living in the present moment and savoring summertime in all her glory. Summer extended beyond the Autumnal Equinox this year here in Boston. It's been unseasonably warm and humid. I am ready to embrace change.
I remember when I was in grade school, I was the narrator for our play "Every season has a reason." We've been through many seasons of our lives with the pandemic which has called for resilience, adaptation, flexibility and embracing the ebb and flow of life during these unprecedented times. This Autumn our family is entering a new season with Tom's retirement, Ruth Anne's return to work after healing from a critical illness and new projects on the horizon for me spreading my powerful message of healing, hope and possibility. I am open to the splendor and glory of the Autumn season shaking loose and letting go, allowing infinite possibilities to emerge.

Do you focus on the leaves dying and shudder at winter coming or do you feel your heart fill with joy and gratitude for this moment and feast on their vibrant colors?

Letting Go

Vibrant verdant leaves of summer fade
no longer needed for shade
hot summer sun yields to Autumn's cool breezes
pumpkins and mums
mirroring branches of orange and red splendor
darkness descends at an early hour
inviting my Light to shine.

Steaming mugs of hot beverages
steamy days no more
wrapped up in cozy comforters
counting blessings
as seasons change
Autumn leaves
letting go
revealing beauty of barren branches
pregnant with infinite possibilities
in winter's slumber
I awaken
reborn.

Watching Grass Grow

Dull or boring
perhaps to some
imagine the miracle
spreading seeds on fertile soil
slender thin blades of grass emerge
like a newborn's head of hair
wisps of green

Source planted seeds
wisdom
excellence
joy
abundance
creativity
health and well-being

In the midst of chaos
releasing fear
sowing seeds of faith
tending my tender heart
reaping the harvest of my life
the Universe is poking me to grow
I am grateful.

Catch and Release

Caught in vortex of fear
remember
Divine Love surrounding
with every accelerating footstep
my mind calms
catch fearful thoughts
watching clouds go by
release their grip
water's stillness reflects Autumn vibes.

Catch myself in a state of worry and fear
releasing my past to Source
unleashing abundance of Light and Love
igniting Spirit
running free
unbounded from shackles of anxious thoughts
a knowing smile breaks through
catching my reflection
my shadow only an illusion
Shine on Spirit
shine on!

"I dare you to train for a marathon and not have it change your life." ~Susan Sidoriak

As one of my friend's posted on Facebook on October 2nd, it's been 901 days since the last Boston Marathon. We are now 9 days away from when Boston runs again. It is a surreal time as we try to find our bearings as we sort of emerge from the pandemic. I am reminded of the strength, courage and resilience our city shared in the wake of the 2013 Boston Marathon bombings. We are now in the wake of a pandemic that shook our City and the world to its core. We continue to experience the turbulent currents in our lives.

Why would I stand on my feet for 3 hours helping to stuff the packets that 20,000 runners will receive next weekend when they pick up their bibs, packets and shirts before running Monday's Boston Marathon? I know how I felt when we picked up our packets, bibs and shirts before the 2009 Boston Marathon. It's the final moments leading up to crossing the starting line in Hopkinton. There's the program book filled with history and anticipation along with coupons, spectators' guide and memorabilia to cherish. For everyone, training for a marathon is a journey of transformation. Mine was a journey of transformation on steroids after having been told to prepare to spend the rest of my life in a wheelchair after the diagnosis of Post-Polio Syndrome. Packet stuffing is a wonderful way to give back and celebrate the Boston Marathon.

When we registered to volunteer, we were overjoyed that with vaccinations, we would experience life as we had before the pandemic; hugs, no masks, being together side by side and anticipating one of the premier events in Boston. The emails from the BAA arrived in our inbox talking about safety and precautions along with the need to be vaccinated or have a negative COVID-19 test in order to volunteer. During this time of emerging (sort of) from the pandemic, everyone talks about risk tolerance. I knew everyone would be vaxed or tested, masked and the packet stuffing takes place in an open air warehouse. I hadn't seen running family since we hosted the water stop in March of 2020. I knew that any minor risk I was taking with my husband and daughter paled in comparison to the rich rewards of volunteering and seeing friends I had not seen in a very long time.

During my meditation before bed on Saturday night, I remembered how I felt about being a spectator at the BAA 10K in June of 2013. I knew that I could not allow fear to keep me away from my beloved running community - then - or now.

It was quite a different scene at Gentle Giant Warehouse as we stood in line waiting to be checked in with masks up and vaccination cards in hand. The former 'Madam President' (as she is affectionately known) of L Street Running Club greeted us with both her no-nonsense laser focus on the task at hand and such kindness and love in her voice as she checked us off with hands that had beautiful blue and yellow perfectly manicured nails.

Tom Licciardello who has been the leader of the pack for packet stuffing through the decades greeted me with a warm hug.

"How were you able to recognize me with my mask?"

"Oh Mary, I'd recognize you from anywhere!"

His wife Lyn came up and warmly greeted Team McManus.

At packet stuffing in 2014, there were many more volunteers to get packets ready for 36,000 runners versus 20,000 runners for 2021. We had more space between volunteers and of course we all had to wear masks throughout the entire shift. But one thing that didn't change is the love running family shares no matter how much time may have passed since we saw one another, and our deep desire to be a part of the Boston Marathon tradition.

Conversations flow with ease among runners and I was blessed to share my table with a Strider who went to Bermuda one of the years we went for Bermuda Marathon Weekend. It was great to reminisce about a time before; when we could travel to destination races with only our passports and running gear. Music kept us pumped up while we did the tedious work. We tried our best to keep the conversation light although at times our conversation turned to sharing our experiences during the pandemic. I was blessed to have a few heart to heart moments with Tom with whom I have been friends for 12 years. We were tired and happy at the end of our shift knowing that we achieved our goal to have the packets ready for the runners this weekend when they arrive at the Expo. It was glorious to see people in person, sharing the Spirit of the Boston Marathon remembering that we ARE Boston Strong.

Oh Boston Marathon How I Missed Thee
October 12, 2021

"There is a unique energy surrounding the Boston Marathon that you can't help but feel. It includes every runner and every person along the course. It brings every person together as one." ~Amy Hastings

I woke up at 5am on Marathon Monday to go to the bathroom. We live less than 2 miles from the course as it runs along Beacon Street. I felt the electric energy that began last week reach its peak. I could not get back to sleep despite my best meditation efforts. I basked in the anticipation of the Boston Marathon that had not happened since April 15, 2019 which also marked the 6th anniversary of the Boston Marathon bombing. I finally fell asleep for another hour after we fed our cat at 6:30.

You would think that Team McManus was running Boston again as we anxiously ate our breakfast and prepared to combine our Monday morning miles with watching the Marathon. True to Team McManus form we bantered back and forth about the best routes and plan for the day which often happened during our training runs for the 2009 Boston Marathon. We decided to go first to Cleveland Circle to see the wheelchair runners. Our pre-COVID-19 routine would have been to pack a cooler and head out early with our chairs to the corner of Dean Road and Beacon Street. I must say I enjoyed the change of being on foot and experiencing Marathon Monday in a novel way.

We let Spirit guide where to go next and got in our miles en route to Dean Road and Beacon Street in time to see elite runners and cheer for the wheelchairs and hand cycles. We were fortunate to see Nell Rojas. She was the first American woman to finish and finished 6th overall. We waited to see if we could cheer on Desi Linden who was the champion in 2018 during torrential downpours. The crowd cheered as loudly for her as if she were the leader.

As all good runners know, it is vital to pace, fuel and hydrate. We returned home to give our legs a rest after 3.35 miles of mostly hills while continuing to track our friends.

We miraculously found a parking spot not far from Beacon Street. We carried our chairs for the long afternoon of cheering on our friends to the finish line. Because there were fewer runners and spectators, and with the new app that was great for tracking beyond the usual notifications at different points along the course, we were able to find our friends among the sea of runners. Air hugs and blowing kisses replaced the traditional hugs, high fives and cheek kissing, as Spirits were flying high. The joy, the love, the unity among spectators and runners brought healing to a people and City. I am sure the reverberations were felt around the Globe. What unbridled joy we felt to see friends in person.

I was blessed to see Ben Beach who went on to finish his 54th consecutive Boston Marathon in spite of living with dystonia. We shared a panel for the Virtual Boston Marathon Expo last year on Late Life Running and Whole Life Running.

There were so many inspiring stories from the day.

Bret Parker lives with Parkinson's Disease. He runs to raise money and awareness to find a cure for Parkinson's Disease. I was thrilled he wore a t-shirt that said "Give Bret some love" so we could cheer loudly for him as he passed by. He told me on Facebook that he was sorry he couldn't stop because he was going for a sub-7 hour marathon which he accomplished. Team Babsie went on to make history as the first mother-daughter duo in the Boston Marathon. I met Beth at another race two years ago and we've become friends in social media and in real life. The circle of love and inspiration grows with Team Hoyt at the hub of the racing duos accomplishments. Beth's mother lives with Multiple Sclerosis and they followed in the footsteps of Dick and Rick Hoyt enabling Beth's mom to feel a sense of freedom while Beth pushed her in a duo wheelchair.

One of our friends, Michelle Marchese Corrado was slowly making her way to the finish line. She was well trained and ready to run the April 2020 Boston Marathon. She did not want to run the Virtual event even though she met her fundraising and training goals. She signed on to run the 2021 Boston Marathon for the Cam Neely Foundation. Can you imagine going through a year and a half of training and fundraising? She was fierce and determined in her fundraising and running goals. Several weeks before Boston, she experienced severe calf cramping. She would not give up and harnessed the help of acupuncture to add to her massage therapy and ramped up cross training regimen. We were going to go back out to cheer her on to the finish when the app said she could not be located.

We prayed. I knew that she was not going to stop unless there was a health risk. The day was getting cooler and I knew she was only wearing a singlet. We continued to pray and we prayed for her health and safety, for being able to finish and just as important that there would be someone there to give her the medal! Between the two charities from whom she received bibs, she raised over $20,000 for charities that support cancer patients and their families.

At around 7:00pm I went to her Facebook page to see if there was any update.

There it was! The picture of her with her finisher's medal.

Ruth Anne and I cried and hugged each other.

Yesterday's Boston Marathon was so much bigger than Marathon Monday. It was a day that a community of runners, spectators and a City came alive. The longest training cycle ever came to an end.

While many aspects of Marathon Monday were different, there was a game played at Fenway Park as happens when the Marathon is run on Patriots Day. The stars aligned and the Red Sox are off to play in the American League Championship Series!

It was the perfect ending to a magnificent day! Oh Boston Marathon how I've missed thee but fortunately we only have to wait 6 months for the 2022 Boston Marathon to happen again in April.

"Watching the world's best compete fires you up to achieve your own feats of greatness. When it comes to running, participation and spectating go hand in hand.". ~Kara Goucher

"I still remember the days I prayed for the things I have now."
~Anonymous

Fifteen years ago this week with voice and hands trembling, I reached out to Spaulding Rehab's International Rehab Center for Polio and Post-Polio Syndrome to take the first very tentative steps on my healing journey. As I wrote in "Coming Home: A Memoir of Healing, Hope and Possibility":

The buzzing hum from the fluorescent lights echoed the buzzing in my nervous system. I sat waiting for my first appointment at the post-polio clinic at the IRCP. My complexion was as white as the paper that covered the exam table. I felt as fragile and vulnerable as that piece of paper that gets ripped off and tossed away after the exam. Every inch of my body hurt. I was exhausted. I was sick and tired of feeling sick and tired. I hadn't really cared whether or not I woke up in the morning but I had a husband and twins that needed me. Ironically enough I was at the peak of my career as a VA social worker. I couldn't sleep. I felt depressed. My award-winning career as a social worker at the Department of Veterans Affairs no longer fueled my soul. Somewhere deep inside of me there was a feeling that there had to be a way out of the hell I was living in.

The symptoms began in 1996. I had episodes of feeling fatigue and muscle burning. I was anxious. At times, I noticed that the limp from paralytic polio returned. In 1992, I had reconstructive leg surgery to correct the deformity of my left leg and to avoid a total knee replacement at the young age of 39 years old. Here I was several years later feeling as though my body was beginning to deteriorate and my life falling apart.

Today, as I was carrying the laundry from the 2nd floor to the basement, I reflected on how I felt 15 years ago. I could barely walk up one flight of stairs let alone carry a laundry basket. After exhaustive diagnostic testing, the diagnosis of Post-Polio Syndrome was made. I pleaded with the Occupational Therapist to help me work for 3 more years until I would be eligible for retirement.

"You must give up the life you planned in order to have the life that is waiting for you." ~Joseph Campbell

I did not take kindly to being dependent on my family members. I was a Type A personality on steroids. I knew I needed to leave my award-winning career as a VA social worker. The Team at Spaulding said if there were any chance of stabilizing the symptoms where they were, I had to consider leaving my career. I needed to use a toe up leg brace, a cane and a wheelchair for mobility whenever I needed to travel long distances and to confront the reality that I would probably need to spend the rest of my life in a wheelchair.

There was a possibility I would need a feeding tube given that the left side of my esophagus was sluggish and causing me to aspirate food into my lungs. They recommended a sleep apnea machine at night to try to improve my breathing since my lungs were not operating at full capacity as a result of the paralytic polio. I refused. In February, I got still and asked for Divine Guidance. I did not like where my life was heading and knew I had to do something if I were going to have a life.

I knew that my mind, body and soul were crying out for healing from the effects of paralytic polio and severe childhood trauma.

We used Pea Pod for grocery deliveries. I started to journal and focused on gratitude. And then a portal to healing opened wide as my pen became my divining rod for healing. Poetry poured out of me visualizing a future very different than the ones the Team predicted for me. Poetry was a powerful vehicle to also heal my past.

Forgiveness, faith and gratitude were the lynch pins during those early days of my healing journey as I feverishly wrote poetry channeled through Spirit to take me on a journey of miraculous healing.

I continue to practice an attitude of gratitude and know that every step is a gift and every mile I continue to run is a blessing. I no longer have the tub chair, the cane, the toe up leg brace or the wrist splint that were prescribed for me. I feel the joy of being able to grocery shop even though we still have to wear masks and be socially distant when we do.

It's been fifteen years since my first visit to Spaulding and the diagnosis that would set me on a journey of miraculous transformation. I remember how I asked for Divine Guidance to help lift me out of the dark night of my mind, body and soul. I remember the days when I prayed for everything I am so blessed to experience now!

Faring Well

Facing fears
dread dripping like candle's hot wax
must not let it snuff out my light
it's time to bid farewell my dear
past is past
I passed the tests
transform thoughts
fare well with happiness and health
peace and prosperity
abundance
relief
comfort
at ease
butterfly on the breeze
sweet nectar of life
now flows.

As the pandemic continues to be ever present in our lives, and rancor and bitterness continues in Washington, I pray that there will come a day when we look back at this time feeling healed and whole. I pray that we can come together as individuals, as communities and as a global community to emerge from the pandemic into the light feeling grateful that what we once prayed for has come to pass. I know a time will come in the not too distant future when we will look back on *this* time with gratitude for soul lessons learned.

Into the Light

Emerging From the Pandemic: From FOMO to Let's Go
October 25, 2021

I saw the social media posts of reopening night of "Jagged Little Pill" with comments made by people with their dates of when they were going to see the show. My friends from Voices of Hope were among them. I talked with Tom and Ruth Anne about whether or not we should go. With COVID-19 and the need to mask everywhere we once again said we would wait until Springtime. My friends totally understood but then one of my friend's sent me a message on Facebook letting me know that a member of Voices of Hope had two tickets available and connected us with the ticket holder.

Okay Universe .... You really want us to go to New York and be a part of this experience. In hind sight, I realized we were all experiencing COVID-19 fatigue. We'd been irritable and feeling down. We were used to having events to look forward to and it seemed as though we had reached our limit of not having anything on the calendar (or anything on our fridge) to look forward to. We enjoyed our Boston Marathon experience that seemed to ignite that desire within us to not let the parade pass us by (referencing a wonderful number from Hello Dolly!)

We were able to book a room where our friends will be staying and bought tickets in the mezzanine. Everyone will be vaccinated or test negative for COVID-19, and I will take these next 4 weeks to mentally prepare for rocking my mask in NYC, harnessing the power of visualization to find a space of ease. I always make a list of things we must remember before going on any trip. It was trippy to put vaccination cards and masks on the list. I trust the vaccine. I trust masks, and I trust my body's immune system. I know that feeling joyful and being with people who embody love is good for the immune system. The time has come to face the fear, ditch the fear, and anticipate a New York City experience as the lights go back on Broadway.

it's about learning to dance or as I like to say it's about learning to run in the rain!

We were spoiled by mild temperatures and sunshine for most of the month of October. As I do every year, I take time to savor being able to sit in the yard or at the park in warm sunshine and heading out the door in t-shirts and shorts or capris. This year, summer was extended well into October and the running was easy. I was thrilled that the high heat and humidity were gone and we could enjoy being outdoors, taking deep breaths and seeing the green leaves linger on the trees, along with the glow on my face and tan lines on my legs and shoulders. It seemed as though we went from temperatures in the 60's and 70's with sunshine and gentle breezes to 50's with gusty winds and rain. We have a treadmill in our basement which is reserved for those days when it is absolutely not safe to run outdoors.

On the first day of chilly rain, Ruth Anne and I had an "oh I really don't want to do this" moment to "Let's go." We know that mental attitude is everything and so we smiled as we headed out the door with an ooh it's chilly expression that quickly transformed into smiles of joy and gratitude. We debated about where to run and started out with a 'neighborhood run.' We decided it wasn't 'too bad' and went to the Reservoir where we were treated to a different beauty from when there are blue skies and sunshine. Ruth Anne and I know a time when we weren't able to get outdoors and share a run together; when I was finding my healing path after the diagnosis of Post-Polio Syndrome and when she was finding her healing path in the wake of PANDAS/PANS. We feel deeply blessed and grateful that we are healed. Whatever the weather, the fact we are *able* to get outdoors on a run is an incredible gift!

On Wednesday, the weather called for gusty winds and torrential rain. The weather forecast recommended that people move to the lower level of their homes for safety and stay indoors. Driving would be hazardous and treacherous. During breakfast, as we debated what to do, we leaned toward taking turns on the treadmill, blaring our favorite music and cheering each other on. We kept opening and closing the door as if that would change the weather. The winds had not yet picked up and the rain was a steady drizzle. We remembered what runners say, "There is no such thing as bad weather, only bad running gear."

We layered up and opted for the neighborhood run knowing the gusts coming off the water at the Reservoir would have been too intense. We ended up doing 3.28 miles because we missed the turnaround at the halfway mark. We are once again getting acclimated to running in all kinds of weather. Thanks to the pandemic, we had the opportunity to get outside for our runs in all sorts of weather because gyms were closed. We know the benefits of cold air, being outdoors, and the joy of triumph over the elements. The storm hit hard and the South Shore of Massachusetts experienced widespread electrical outages and severe flooding. We usually lose electricity during storms while our neighbors are fine because we are on a different grid, but we were so fortunate to have electricity and heat while the storm raged on.

We enjoyed hot cocoa and the sweet satisfaction of not sitting and waiting for the storm to pass. Life is about learning how to dance...and run in the storms regardless of circumstances!

For the first time in over a week, the sun finally broke through the clouds here in New England. Clean up continued after the Nor'Easter that was classified as a hurricane. The Cape Cod Marathon Race Weekend was cancelled and emergency crews worked 24/7 to restore electricity, yet there was still a feeling of joy and anticipation for Halloween. Even before COVID-19, after our own children were grown, we would always ask the question, "Should we do Halloween this year?" Our neighborhood, as many neighborhoods tend to do, go through cycles of having younger children. We live near a school and families move in with younger children and leave once children are grown making room for younger families to move in again. The group of old homesteaders like Tom and me are rare these days.

Halloween has never been one of my favorite holidays but experiencing it through the eyes of our twins was always a joy. I loved when they did trick or treat for UNICEF. This year, at the last minute we decided to have treats on hand and trusted, as Dr. Ingrid Katz noted in a boston.com article that Halloween is really quite a safe holiday.

We received a last minute invitation from our neighbors to attend an outdoor party with pizza for the kids and 'adult beverages.' We politely declined as Tom and Ruth Anne are training for a marathon and were tired after their long run. Their house abuts our property and the party overflowed into our yard. There were kids in costumes running around, shrieking with delight that they were able to celebrate Halloween this year while adults stood in close proximity to one another without masks socializing, enjoying the opportunity to have a party. We sent out positive energy that everyone would remain safe and healthy.

Given the throngs of children and adults that were lining our street, we decided on a contactless Halloween this year. We hung the bag of treats from the railing on our porch and greeted the Trick or Treaters through our storm door reminding them to please take only one treat each. We were astounded by the numbers of children and adults out and about. Our treats were gone within an hour. We usually have left overs that we'd bring into work the next day.

This year's Halloween celebration was far more than the hunger for sweets; everyone is hungering for a return to rituals and celebrations without the pandemic. Yet the pandemic still hangs like a scepter over everyone. The White House Press Secretary, Jen Psaki, tested positive for COVID-19 after family members tested positive and reported mild symptoms. She was unable to accompany the President to the G20 summit which is addressing climate change; another crisis happening in the world right now.

We need to shine our lights more brightly than ever before as we move toward the Winter Solstice. We cannot wait for the light to slowly return. It is a time to set aside judging what others are choosing to do and focus on making choices that are right for us. It is time to shine the light on gratitude and blessings. It is a time to go within for contemplation allowing the darkness to surround us but not engulf us, and find the gifts in this glorious time of year.

In the Darkness

I wrap myself in a blanket
cozy and warm
sipping hot cocoa
eyes half closed
a time for contemplation.

Overcoming fears and worries
casting a light on all there is to be grateful for
thanksgiving a holiday every day
fasting from fears
feasting on faith.

Out of the darkness of my past
I am transformed
a light bearer
having borne many battles
fighting for my soul.

Stillness and listening
Spirit pierces veil
revealing Truth and Knowledge
every problem solved
embracing beauty of stars
they can only be seen in the darkness.

Celebrating 15 Years of Healing: A Contemplative Run
November 5, 2021

"Reaching far beyond my limitations internally through contemplation allowed me to reach beyond my limitations externally through running." ~Michael D'Aulerio

It's sometimes hard for me to fathom that it's been 15 years since I first took steps on my healing journey emerging from the dark night of my mind, body and soul. I have faint memories of how awful I felt in the Autumn and early Winter of 2006-2007. I am in awe of the miracle of healing. My healing work began with tapping into my imagination and seeing beyond appearances of needing a toe up leg brace, a cane and at times a wheelchair for mobility. I was told to prepare to spend the rest of my life in a wheelchair. My pen became my Divining rod for healing as poetry flowed out of me inspiring mind, body and soul to heal my past through forgiveness and gratitude, creating a future of healing, wholeness and being free in my body.

Wednesday was an absolutely glorious Autumn day. As Tom and Ruth Anne train for the Providence Marathon, my runs these days are solo runs. I luxuriate in the solitude and a time for contemplation and reflection while I soak in the sights, sounds and scents of Autumn in New England.

Tom started a new contract job 3 weeks ago. After exploring the two job offers, he received, he realized he did not want the stress of a full time job for now. It was supposed to be fully remote with a one or two day a month commute to New Hampshire but it was an everyday or 2-3 times a week commute to New Hampshire. Aside from the time of the commute, we are a one car family. There were issues with Tom's payroll and accessing his laptop from home. I turned it all over to Source and asked for guidance as I had 15 years ago when I had been diagnosed with Post-Polio Syndrome. It can be so easy to try and control everything with an iron fist rather than open my hands to grace and guidance.

On Monday, our wall oven wouldn't turn on. I had trouble getting an appointment to have a GE repairman come out while also looking for a replacement oven. Our oven is over 10 years old or so I believed, Everything was on back order and our oven is no longer manufactured. My mind started racing about what would happen for Thanksgiving, was there another option, maybe we should plan Thanksgiving with our son. But with each footstep my stress was relieved and I had to trust that somehow everything would work out.

I was able to exchange kindness and compassion with people I had contact with to secure a new wall oven and the steps necessary to get the space measured before accepting the delivery. One woman told me that she wished every customer was like me. I remembered how I felt out on my run and let those feelings fuel my negotiations as I navigated a COVID-19 world fraught with supply chain issues and staffing shortages. I watched the magic happen as an appointment with a GE technician opened up for this morning. It just happened to be a technician we have known through the years. He worked his magic and was able to repair the oven. He looked up the information about our oven and informed us it was only two years old! We could renew our service protection plan. He also did not charge us for parts stating that they were under warranty.

There were moments earlier in the week when I felt completely overwhelmed. Tom experienced the stress of starting a new role in combination with the commute. Ruth Anne started working part-time for the Town of Brookline which is a magnificent milestone in her healing journey but she had to be at work by 7:45. When I felt that solar plexus clutch and adrenaline rush of worry, I would take a few minutes to sit down, look at the beautiful photos I took out on the run, breathe deeply and trust that we would always find a way to manage everything. I focused on all the blessings in our lives and as I did 15 years ago, let my pen be my Divining rod for healing:

Make It Easy on Yourself

When times seem tough
make it easy on yourself
connect to Source!

Outsource worries and fears

When ease seems hard to find
feel faith coursing through your veins
allowing grace to reign
showering you with Divine Love.

Angels seen and unseen stand at the ready
struggles cease
challenges transform
exhale a sigh of relief
with belief and trust.

Ease now flows
sitting by the river bank
nature our best teacher
rustling of autumn leaves
a reminder to let go.

Ease up
look up
and within and around
all is well
be at peace
be at ease.

As I write this, the smell of Superhero Muffins from Shalane Flanagan's cookbook fills the air. I can plan meals to cook in the oven and we don't have to rely on our grill or our cook top for sustenance. Tom worked out a plan for primarily working from home with his manager. Ruth Anne is thrilled with her part-time job and feels a deep sense of accomplishment for being back at work and making her way in the world once more.

Wednesday's contemplative run was exactly what I needed to reset my mind, body and soul. I have come so far in my healing journey during these past 15 years and I have to be extremely mindful to not allow unhealthy patterns repeat themselves. When stress bears down in the midst of a pandemic, it can be challenging to not revert to old coping mechanisms. Thanks to the gift of running in my life, and the wisdom I have garnered during these past 15 years, I was able to ultimately successfully navigate circumstances beyond my control.

It's Been Awhile - Countdown to NYC - The Joy of Anticipation
November 9, 2021

"Anticipation makes pleasure more intense." ~*Iris Johansen*

When I received the email confirming our reservations from Mama Mia, a classic New York City Italian Restaurant within walking distance of our hotel and the theater district, I felt an intense mix of emotions! The last time I took out a suitcase to pack was in February of 2020 for the Hyannis Marathon Weekend. My suitcases would be rolled in and out of the closet at least several times a year. We did destination race weekends and traveled to Cape Cod and Bermuda for vacations. There was quite a bit of dust around the wheels from its lack of use. I'm the type of person who starts packing about two weeks in advance checking things off of our to pack list. Our blue carry on suitcase that we will use for our overnight trip to New York is just standing in our bedroom.

I'm almost at a loss for how to proceed because it's been so long since we've gone on an overnight trip. After we were fully vaxed, we began to make plans and anticipate events and travel with great joy. And then came the Delta Variant and a new set of guidelines. Do I allow myself to fully experience the anticipation of a road trip, experiencing the joy of the city that never sleeps and a Broadway show? Can I allow myself to think about the luxury of not having to cook or clean for 48 hours, being with wonderful, loving friends and savoring the sights, sounds and smells of New York right before the holidays?

I've made a conscious decision to say YES to experiencing the joy of anticipation.

The New York City Marathon was held yesterday. My friends posted photos of the Expo and taking in the sights of New York before race day. You could feel the electric energy of Times Square through cyberspace. Several of my friends posted that they burst their bubble with the New York City Marathon Weekend. Many of my friends have already traveled, gone to the theater and movies and dined at restaurants. I may be a little late to the party but I am emerging from the pandemic in my own way and in my own time teasing out what risks we want to take. Writing this, I realize that I have not been away from my house for any length of time since February of 2020. It continues to feel surreal. Travel used to be an integral part of our lives. We settled into a life without travel or running events. We focused on being present, navigating the uncharted course of circumstances way beyond our control and doing the best we could to experience life to the full despite the pandemic.

Boston Marathon Weekend was our first introduction back into a world beyond our family. My soul felt nourished by the adventure of meeting new people and cheering on friends on Marathon Monday. The world has changed and shifted but our resilience and strength shine through. Broadway's lights were dimmed for many months. Starting lines were quiet. Hotels and airports were vacant. Many businesses pivoted or sadly closed. Restaurants had to pivot to take out windows. Loved ones were separated by oceans as international travel was halted.

Today, international travel to the United States resumed, and the front page of the Boston Globe showed emotional photos of loved ones being reunited in airports. I can only imagine the joy they felt in anticipation of reunions. International travelers are being welcomed back to the theater, although the Broadway League announced today that pandemic guidelines are being extended through February 28th.

On April 22nd, when Sean Allan Krill was a guest on Voices of Hope Boston's podcast, The Cardinal Café, he spoke with hosts Greg and Ed about the anticipation of the re-opening of Broadway in the Fall. They were setting up vaccine sites to help get the theaters open again. They talked about what it was like during the first few weeks of the pandemic when it looked like a post-apocalyptic movie. Sean went on to say, "It's not like that now. There are more people coming to New York just to visit. I'm not sure if that's good or bad but I do believe we are on the right track. Thank God for the vaccines and that we are working towards getting to the point where we can all sit in a big room together and enjoy something."

Ed chimed in, 'We just have to get past the Spring break surge."

"Exactly, exactly," Sean said.

"Well you just better be ready Sean because when things open up you're gonna have, I bet we're gonna have at least 50-75 of our members (referencing Voices of Hope Boston) who are gonna be on the bus, on the train and the first show we are going to see is "Jagged Little Pill"," Ed replied.

"Wow I can't wait," Sean said with such warmth and love in his voice. "You're gonna let me know. You're gonna let me know, right? They probably won't have a line for a while and nobody will be able to come backstage but I can certainly come out."

Sean went on to say, "It sounds crazy to even talk about it. I know it's not impossible but at this point a year in it does feel like, Wow, is that ever really going to happen? But let's plan that. It sounds really nice."

It's time to unzip the suitcase and begin putting in items we are going to need for our first adventure since the pandemic began. I printed out driving directions. Ruth Anne, Tom and I plotted out where we want to go during our first trip back to New York with walking directions to get there. I went shopping in my closet to find clothes to wear to the theater. Seven months after Greg and Ed talked about a group of Voices of Hope members (of which I am an honorary member) heading to New York to see "Jagged Little Pill", I am counting down to our NYC return. I am savoring every moment of the joy of anticipation. I know it's going to be better than I could have ever imagined in my wildest dreams.

"Joy is the most magnetic force in the Universe." ~Danielle LaPorte

There comes a moment when you just let go and allow joy to happen. After Friday morning's meditation, I felt a stirring in my soul. I asked Team McManus what they thought about seeing if we could get our hotel room a day early and head to NYC to thoroughly enjoy the experience and be rested for Saturday night when we had tickets to see "Jagged Little Pill". Tom and Ruth Anne were ecstatic. Nine phone calls later, our hotel room was booked for Friday night. I kept getting bounced back between the place where I originally booked the reservation and the hotel. I wondered if it was a sign we weren't meant to leave on Friday but then I received an agent who helped me schedule the room for Friday.

While Ruth Anne was at work and Tom worked from home, I went into high gear getting everything ready and packed up for our New York City adventure. Tom finished his work from home day at 3:30. We hoped to be on the road by 4 with a stop in Providence for dinner.

We were on our way to our first vacation since Hyannis Marathon Weekend in February of 2020!

We didn't account for traffic on a Friday afternoon heading to New York City. Our plan for a stop in Providence was quickly changed as we literally went around in circles trying to access 95 South according to "Google girl" helping us find the fastest route. We were treated to a spectacular sunset which reminded us to focus on the bigger picture rather than the frustration of being stuck in traffic. We changed the destination from Providence to our NYC hotel and decided we'd stop at a place along the way. We put our faith in "Google girl" to somehow redirect us and get us to New York some time before midnight which was when our reservation would no longer be valid. I told reservations we planned to arrive some time around 9pm.

We found a service plaza on the Mass. Pike, donned our masks and explored our options. We decided on Cheesy Street Grill where two gentlemen worked hard to keep their area clean and serve up sandwiches to their customers. There was an intensity and dedication to their work. We decided that we were meant to eat there, give these two servers a really good tip and tell them how awesome they were. The sandwiches were delicious and we were ready to go the distance with destination New York City.

Fortunately the traffic was light and we made it to New York just before 10. We unpacked the car and Tom took the car to the parking garage where we would receive validated parking after check out. He arrived back at the room and we were so relieved we made it. We were ready to get a good night's sleep with a full day in New York on Saturday.

I asked Tom where our cooler was with our water bottles, sparkling water and fruit. "Oh shoot. I left it at the car," he said.

"No problem," I said. "We will get it tomorrow."

"Um no. We can't. They take your car and park it and you can't get to it until you're ready to leave."

I watched him go through his pockets and asked him what he was looking for.

"Oh no. I must have dropped the receipt!"

He went back and fortunately there was a wonderful attendant who not only replaced the receipt but went to the car to get the cooler.

We all settled down with meditation to quell the adrenaline of the excitement for what Saturday's adventures would bring!

"Believe in the magic of Christmas." ~Macy's

The magic of Christmas is synonymous with New York. There's the Thanksgiving Day Macy's Parade which always ends with the entrance of Santa Claus, the holiday classic Miracle on 34th Street, Radio City Music Hall and the Rockettes, and of course, ice skating at Rockefeller Center with the spectacular Christmas Tree. While the tree was lit last year and there was a pre-taped Parade, it was very difficult to experience the magic of Christmas in New York and around the world. While many decked the halls of our homes on Thanksgiving with Christmas decorations, it was a challenge to feel the light and hope of the winter holidays surrounded by so much darkness and fear.

One year later we are emerging from the pandemic and New York City seemed to shine more brightly than it ever has. We were so blessed to be there before the crowds descended on the City and while the air was filled with the festivities of the holiday season.

We woke up early on Saturday morning to the setting moon. We took time to meditate before heading out on what we knew would be a whirlwind shopping and walking tour of the City. We didn't know just how much of a walking tour we would experience!

After breakfast at the Majestic Delicatessen, we went to the M&M store where Ruth Anne wanted to bring back gifts for her co-workers who keep a supply of M&M's at their desks. We saw windows decorated for Christmas. When Ruth Anne asked me what I wanted to do in New York, I told her I wanted to take lots of pictures of her and of all of us being together. I wanted to celebrate being on our first vacation since February 2020 and the miracle of her healing from a traumatic brain injury.

After experiencing the magic of the M&M store, Ruth Anne proudly sported her M&M shopping bag over her shoulder while we walked to Rockefeller Center.

Even though the scaffolding was still on the tree while workers strung the lights and trimmed branches, the magic of Christmas filled the air. We stopped in the NBC Studio Store but it was a shadow of its former self. The Plaza in front of the NBC studios that would have people with their noses pressed to the glass watching the Today Show was empty. Yet there was a powerful sense of resilience and strength pulsating throughout the City. Our beloved restaurant, Cucina Cucina was closed apparently as a result of the pandemic.

By contrast, Radio City Music Hall was buzzing with excitement as throngs of people lined up to present their proof of vaccination or negative COVID-19 test and ID's to see the Holiday Show. We made a stop at St. Patrick's Cathedral where we traditionally light a candle. I welled up with emotion to realize that when we were there with friends 5 years ago, we lit a candle for Ruth Anne who was critically ill. She lit a candle and we tightly hugged each other.

We were going to be up very late since we were going to the 8pm show of "Jagged Little Pill". We are typically not late night people so we wanted to pace our day and headed back to the hotel. I grew up in Westchester and would often take the train into the City to meet my great Aunt Laura. She taught me how New York is a grid and took great care to explain how to navigate getting around the City on foot. That was long before the days of GPS and iPhones. Tom put on "Google girl" to direct us back to the hotel. I should have trusted my instincts and paid attention to where we were going. By the time I spoke up about going in the wrong direction, we were another mile away from our hotel.

It felt so good to put our feet up and rest before heading out for lunch. We heard about Junior's from many of our friends who visited New York. It exceeded our expectations with service and food. We were planning to have lighter fare for lunch and have dinner at Mama Mia's before the show. After perusing the menu and seeing what people were eating, we decided to have a 'lunner'; a combination of lunch and dinner. Because of our detour, it was already 1:30.

It was incredible to feel my Jewish roots and savor traditional Jewish food in New York. Before heading back to the hotel, we went to see the marquis for "Jagged Little Pill". We felt the excitement build and the thrill of the lights being back on Broadway!

When we arrived back at the hotel at about 3:30, our friends from Voices of Hope Boston were checking in. They were preparing for their Spring gala in March of 2020 when life came to a screeching halt. We would see our Voices of Hope Boston friends at least twice a year at their shows. It was an emotional reunion. Even though we wore masks, the love and joy were overwhelming as we hugged one another.

We left them to check in while we went to our room to rest before it was time for the show!

"Jagged Little Pill": Seeds of Possibilities Blossomed
November 24, 2021

"Hope lies in dreams, in imagination, and in the courage of those who dare to make dreams into reality." ~Jonas Salk

After we rested in our hotel room, we got dressed and walked over to the Broadhurst Theater with our vaccine cards and photo ID's in hand to get in line for "Jagged Little Pill."

The line moved quickly. We were greeted with, "Welcome back to Broadway," from everyone who greeted us at the theater. We stopped to get a soda water.

"Where's the designated area to drink?" I asked the concession stand person.

"Oh you can take the drinks to your seats now! And there are free refills so feel free to come back for more."

We climbed the stairs to the mezzanine and kept saying to each other, "I can't believe we're really here."

We bought our tickets on October 24th many weeks after the Voices of Hope Boston group bought their tickets yet we were seated a row behind our friends. What a thrilling way to experience the lights being back on Broadway. We filled three and a half rows of the center of the mezzanine!

At intermission, we shared the experience of the First Act with our Voices of Hope family. Ed said to us. "Buckle up for Act Two." He had seen Jagged when it was performed at the American Repertory Theater in Cambridge.

He was right!

There were many moments where I welled up and rode the emotions in awe of the music, the script and the entire theatrical experience.

After the scene where MJ overdoses, my legs trembled. I tried to stop them but then I remembered Peter Levine's book, "In An Unspoken Voice-How the Body Releases Trauma and Restores Goodness." When a body that has experienced trauma, feels overwhelming emotions it can be released through trembling and it's a very healthy way to heal. After the show I stood up for the standing ovation. It ordinarily takes me a few minutes to get my energy flowing after sitting for a while but I bounced out of my chair, and bounded down the stairs with such ease after the show! I felt light and free.

Sharing the experience with my daughter and our circle of love in Voices of Hope who prayed for her when she was critically ill for several years was incredibly powerful soul medicine. We had no idea what the outcome would be when Ruth Anne's diagnosis eluded the medical establishment. Dana, who is a nurse, was my rock through that time. She hugged us after the show and said how great it was to see the power of prayer! I thanked her for all of her love and support. "We're family and that's what we do." There were more hugs.

One of the most painful parts of Ruth Anne's traumatic brain injury was that listening to music triggered audio hallucinations. She LOVES music and it was so painful for both of us that we couldn't share it as we waited for her brain to heal. BUT the brain does heal - albeit slowly and so we started reintroducing music into her life. One of her teachers in high school played "Jagged Little Pill" all the time in the copy center where she worked as part of her curriculum. After Sean's interview on the Cardinal Café podcast, we decided to get the vinyl (rather than listening through headphones on her phone) and it was a total success! We used to go to concerts and Broadway in Boston shows. I thought that experience might have been lost forever but I held onto hope. Saturday night we rekindled the experience of being together for live musical theater.

Ruth Anne had to get up at 6am on Monday to get to work so we did not stay to wait for Sean to come down to greet the group but we enjoyed the photos posted on Facebook. It was a thrill to experience the hustle and bustle of the group heading to the Schubert Alley to meet Sean while we headed back to the hotel.

Eliza, one of the members of Voices of Hope said, "He is such an incredibly talented performer and such a beautiful soul."

This was borne out after I sent an email to Sean about my experience at the show.

Hi Mary,

I was so moved reading your email; thank you for sharing your story with me. I'm so grateful to be a part of "Jagged Little Pill" for many reasons, but first and foremost because it seems to affect people in such a visceral way, and (hopefully) offers help. Even if there is just the tiniest opening up lines of communication, understanding, catharsis - it makes it all worth it. I'm sure you feel the same way about the reactions to your beautiful poetry.

Sorry we didn't get to meet in person, but of course I totally understand the necessity for proper care for your daughter.

I hope you and yours have the happiest of holidays!

Love and light,
Sean

Hope planted seeds of possibilities seven months ago and they blossomed at the Broadhurst Theater and the Schubert Alley on Saturday in New York City. I am so grateful I set aside all my concerns about having to wear a mask throughout the weekend, waiting in line to enter the theater and whether or not I could enjoy New York with the COVID-19 regulations. We experienced the magic of New York City at Christmas time and a magical evening of theater as we continue to emerge from the pandemic.

"Christmas waves a magic wand over the world and behold everything is softer and more beautiful." ~Norman Vincent Peale

After a wonderful night's sleep with hearts overflowing with love and gratitude, we woke up for our final morning in New York. Tom and Ruth Anne had work early on Monday morning. While they rested, I organized and packed up our room. We walked over to Junior's for breakfast. There was a long line and we were about to find another place to eat but I suggested we see how long the wait was. As we went to the hostess desk, people were being told they would receive a text when their table was ready. After we showed our vaccination cards and ID's, they led us to a table for 3. We bobbed and weaved through the crowd with our masks still on and were led to a table with the same waitress who served us lunch on Saturday. We feasted on a New York style breakfast with bagels, eggs, French toast and orange juice. We shared our plates with each other and took a picture of the Christmas tree to add to our photo album.

With a noon check out, we didn't have a lot of time to go gallivanting around the City. Since we all need a little Christmas right now, we walked to Rockefeller Center. I had seen an article about the Show Globes in Times Square and was thrilled to see them along with a spectacular view of Times Square keeping my iPhone camera handy to continue to document this historic adventure. We took the traditional selfie with the skating rink in the background. We were blessed with sunny skies and moderate temperatures.

The doorman at FAO Schwarz was making sure that no one entered the store before 11am. They were hosting a special event for the families of fallen firefighters from 9/11. FAO Schwarz always makes me feel like a kid again even though we could only peek through the windows.

While we watched the tree trimming at Rockefeller Center, Tom asked if we could have a cutting from the tree! After we were gifted one of the branches, the security guard told us to wait a minute. He gave us pine cone decorations for another branch! What an incredible way to kick off the holiday season in New York. We were able to enjoy the City before the throngs of holiday goers arrived. Our waitress at Junior's told us the holiday week begins on Monday for New York schools!

Everyone is ready to celebrate this year after a year of darkness and fear. The holidays have a special meaning this year as we get ready to light the lights of our trees, menorahs, Kwanzaa kinara and to celebrate the lights being back on Broadway. Yes, we need a lot of Christmas this year.

Extraordinary

Sunlight sparkles on water
dancing on the gentle ripples
how long we waited to see the sun again
darkness and fear were all pervasive
would light ever prevail

lying in waiting
world's troubles heavy
bearing down on tender hearts
weary as days became months
keep hope alive

Emerging from the pandemic
baby steps
is it safe?
bigger steps
out into the world
leap of faith
at times waiting seemed unbearable

and yet

what joy culminates
sweet experiences that hearts yearned for
ordinary times become extraordinary
hugs pleasure magnified
seeing smiles once more
happy and free
blessed beyond measure.

"Life's roughest storms prove the strength of our anchors."
~Anonymous

There was a strong headwind as I walked out the door for my solo Saturday run. It can be a challenge to feel motivated doing solo runs especially when the weather conditions are far from ideal. I debated about what route I wanted to run knowing that the wind would be particularly strong around the Reservoir with the wind coming off of the water.

I dug deep and something inside of me spurred me on to do the Reservoir run.

I've run in colder temperatures with snow or sleet pelting my face. Today's conditions were mild compared to those. Yet the wind was very powerful. At times I had to work hard to find my balance. I ran around the outer edge of the path to make sure I did not risk falling into the water.

The white caps were intense; quite the contrast to the Reservoir's usual tranquil and serene water.

I soldiered on reflecting on how this run was becoming a wonderful metaphor for life. When there are strong headwinds of challenges, we need to find ways to keep our footing and trust in the strength deep within us. We need to trust our anchor of faith being connected to Source to help us navigate through challenging times.

Saturday's run was a wonderful metaphor for life during COVID-19. The pandemic hit us with full force almost two years ago. We had great difficulty finding equanimity in the midst of the turbulent times. The vaccines brought great hope and, just like on Saturday's run, when the winds died down, I basked in the warmth of the sun and a return to a 'new normal' of life. But before long, we were back in masks and COVID-19 guidelines were reinstated.

———

On Saturday's run, I was struck by how the sun and clouds together looked like an anchor! What relief to be able to shift from survival mode to being able to savor the sunshine and enjoy the beauty of a late Autumn day taking deep breaths to release the stress returning to a state of equilibrium. Rather than bracing against a possible return of strong headwinds, I stayed in the present moment savoring the peace and quiet. I was relaxed and steady when the headwinds reared up and roared once more.

When we are tested by the storms or strong headwinds that come up in our lives, it is a great opportunity to tether our souls to Source. Our anchor of faith is strengthened and we find a strength deep within that lights up for the world to see. I feel blessed and grateful that I knew challenges early in life after contracting paralytic polio and enduring years of trauma at the hands of family members. The wisdom, strength, resilience and resolve I experienced out of those storms helps me to navigate these turbulent times finding my way back to peace and warmth, grateful I am able to hold steady when winds buffet around me.

Autumn Leaves

When Autumn leaves barren branches
bemoaning winter's arrival
Or
revel in joy
bushes bejeweled with blues, reds and greens
lights twinkling
Source winking
awakening with anticipation
eager expectations
unwrapping gift of new days
presence in winter's darkness
glow of Spirits shining with delight
fireplaces warmth a place to gather
cozy and calm wrapped in a soft blanket
swaddled in Love Divine
cat cuddles purring contentment
cocoa's frothy milk
mimics soft snowfall

When autumn leaves
behold beauty
a feast for the senses
fully alive
embracing a new season of life.

"Every habit and pattern I create serves me in some way. When I am ready to let it go, the Universe helps me to release it." ~Louise Hay

There are so many quotes about letting go, moving forward and embracing a New Year. Many of them have negative connotations such as you can't reach for something new if your hands are full of yesterday's junk. Louise Hay's quote is a much gentler and kinder way to look at letting go of what no longer serves us and opening ourselves to embracing the new.

There are many traditions that I've had to let go of during the pandemic. This time of year would be a time to prepare to celebrate the holidays and my Christmas birthday while getting ready for our annual winter trip to Bermuda. This is the 2nd year that we will forego that tradition.

We usually have a slate of races on our calendar as we bid farewell to an old year and head into a New Year including a Jingle Bell run. We have decided to forego the Jingle Bell run this year and stay focused on marathon training. We are not sure if there will be Camp Hyannis aka Hyannis Marathon Weekend which was our last event before the pandemic in March of 2020 but are going to let go of that tradition in 2022. We are hopeful that the Falmouth Road Race and the Cape Cod Marathon will take place in August and October and are excited to return to our happy place for a race-cation. We are very excited about exploring Providence Rhode Island, a new race destination.

There are relationships that we released in 2021 as the pandemic helped us to discern who and what we want to have in our lives. All experiences were an important part of the tapestry of our lives and it's important to honor the importance they served at the time.

Other relationships have flowed into our lives that have brought wonderful rich, new experiences. I was blessed to be a guest on several podcasts to discuss "Hope is a Garden: Poems and Essays

From the 2020 Pandemic" in lieu of in person appearances. In September, Tom realized it was time to retire from his position at Boston College and explore new possibilities. We are now keenly aware of what is important to have in work/life balance. With his technical skills, he will always find a place to work to generate a revenue stream during retirement. We even toyed with a non-technical job but by continuing to work in tech, he is able to do contract jobs and then take time off.

Ruth Anne experienced many different jobs in 2021. As we expressed gratitude for this past year and all we have learned, enjoyed and grown, Ruth Anne was most grateful to discover that she is capable of being able to work and to 'put up with a lot' in the work place. She is discovering her passion and purpose while she pursues her Masters Degree at Boston College. To help manage the symptoms of the traumatic brain injury that occurred as a result of an untreated infection, she was on a complicated medication regimen with many side effects. She is successfully tapering off of these meds and will be going into a New Year with a much lighter and smaller med box having so much more energy and vitality!

While every year brings an ebb and flow of letting go, transition and change, the pandemic has punctuated this cycle with a big exclamation point in 2021.

We don't know if fully vaccinated will mean having a booster shot although trends are heading in that direction. Masks are mandated at least through March of next year. While experts are keeping an eye on trends, Team McManus is keeping their eyes on health, well-being, doing good, letting go and letting in all the goodness and grace of the Universe in 2022. It's a milestone year as Tom turns 70 in March, we celebrate our 44th wedding anniversary and being together 45 years, and the twins turn 35. My intention is to send out ripples of love, kindness, prosperity, abundance and healing from our hearth, hearts and home to the world.

"The subconscious mind cannot tell the difference between what's real and imagined." ~Bob Proctor

Fifteen years ago I harnessed the power of the mind/body connection to heal my life after the diagnosis of Post-Polio Syndrome. Today I find myself harnessing the tools I used then to navigate these challenging times. At this time last year, we thought for sure we would be planning our return trip to Bermuda for Race Weekend. Travel to Bermuda is not recommended. According to CDC guidelines, it is currently a Level 4 destination. A month ago, Bermuda Race Weekend was cancelled. I saw posts from friends traveling to tropical destinations. Knowing I may not have choices about circumstances happening around me, I always have a choice to choose my thoughts and attitude.

Right before I was getting ready to publish my blog this morning, I opened up Lin-Manuel Miranda's book, "G'morning, Gnight! Little pep talks for me & you" to read G'morning as we have done every day since we bought it a few months ago.

G'morning.
This feeling will pass.
These people will pass.
But look at you with the gift of memory.
You can time travel to the good stuff just by
closing your eyes and breathing.
Then come right back to now, eyes up for
the good stuff ahead.
You magic thing.

Synchronicity is beautiful and magical when we allow our hearts and eyes to see beyond what we can touch, see and feel and what is being told to us through the news.

I went through my photos and changed my profile and cover photos on Facebook to photos from Bermuda. I have a photo from the beach as my wallpaper on my iPhone. I allow the joy to flow with my friends' posts allowing my imagination to feel as if I too am in a tropical destination. We've been blessed with the weather in New England for December. I savor every sight of green grass on lawns despite darkness descending earlier every afternoon until the winter solstice next week.

I am an eternal optimist and allow hope to fill my heart and soul despite the headlines.

Fifteen years ago I was given the diagnosis of Post-Polio Syndrome. As I sat in a leg brace using a cane and at times a wheelchair for mobility, I imagined myself dancing and running free. I harnessed the power of my imagination through writing poetry and even though my circumstances looked quite grim at the time, in my mind's eye I was focused on winning a 10K race. I had never run a day in my life yet went on to run the 2009 Boston Marathon.

While part of me feels utterly exhausted from the pandemic; the need for Ruth Anne to be tested and boosted before she returns to grad school at Boston College and the impending regulations that in order to be considered fully vaccinated you need to have a booster shot, I imagine my world free from the pandemic and only needing to remember my bathing suit and running clothes when we travel again. The memories of traveling to Bermuda for many years in December, January, May and July warm my heart and soul. We look through photo albums and reminisce about our adventures in paradise. We remember with so much love the people who are no longer with us in the physical plane but feel their beautiful presence through our hearts and memories. Before I go to sleep at night, after my guided meditation ends, I ask myself where I want to go. I ignite the fire of my imagination and I can almost hear the tree frogs serenading me as I fall asleep. I see the ink from the headlines from the newspaper dripping down the front page while new good news headlines and news stories appear.

We are finding Christmas music old and new that brings us joy and focusing on all there is to be grateful for. Tom found a new 6 month contract job that is 100% remote starting in the New Year. We will be able to take a week's vacation together before he begins his new job and before Ruth Anne starts classes and a part-time job. I am looking forward to a much less frenzied pace of job finding that was a roller coaster ride of emotions as we looked for jobs that were a good fit. I feel the relief as we settle into a routine and rhythm of life.

And while I may not be getting on a plane to travel to our Bermudaful destination where we went for 5 consecutive years in January until the pandemic, I will travel there in my mind's eye, filled with hope that one day we shall return. In the meantime, as I lull myself to sleep, look at my photos, I remind myself how it's the next best thing to being there.

"It is not in numbers but in unity that our great strength lies."
~Thomas Paine

Divisiveness has once again dominated the headlines; a virus that can do more harm than the pandemic. I must say that it is quite easy to find myself 'taking sides' and making judgments about what is right or wrong. I can only do what feels right for me and our family and release making judgments on others' choices lest I contribute to this pandemic of divisiveness.

We were struggling with whether or not to get our booster shots. Ruth Anne's graduate school requires it. We decided to schedule appointments as the studies show that immunity wanes after 6 months. There were boosters required for the polio vaccine and many other vaccines for potentially life threatening illness. In my heart, I know had I not had the polio vaccine, I could have experienced more debilitating symptoms. Collectively we are exhausted from the news of the pandemic especially as we see that Broadway shows have had to cancel performances and restaurants have had to close due to staff testing positive.

It would be easy to focus on the problems.

After the diagnosis of Post-Polio Syndrome, I learned how vital it is to focus on the healing, not on the wounds; on how to make things better rather than focusing on how bad things appear to be.

I started listening to a podcast that I thought would be healing and bring comfort and peace to my quandary about boosters. It only served to leave me scratching my head wondering how is it possible that people criticize people about having immovable opinions which they say are wrong, and yet they are doing the same thing. I turned it off and took a deep breath. I then saw a post that resonated with my heart and soul from Dr. Michael Rocha. He works in New Bedford and dedicates his life to bringing wellness programs to his patients and the community. He started Walk with a Doc in the area, a program promoted by Dr. Vivek Murthy during his first tenure as Surgeon General. He chose to become a physician but continues with his passion for music playing trombone as part of the Buttonwood Brass and Southcoast Brass Band. The latter raises funds for the Boys and Girls Club.

"December 16, 2021
We find ourselves all in an uncomfortable time, again. A prolonged period punctuated by intermittent increases of disease, despair, and disconnect. We are all well beyond what is tolerable regardless of our varied views.

We are seeing our world crumbling again, feeling like we could get together more safely, then cruelly, the virus decides otherwise. We are seeing hospitals fill up and feeling the strain in all areas of medicine. Breakthrough cases are disrupting our lives, work, families, and our holidays.

Everyone is angry and burned out. We must realize in the moment, it doesn't seem like the suffering will get better. It will. Why?

Science and compassion for one another will win out despite our exhaustion. Unfortunately, science in this moment is telling us to be more careful and make some short term sacrifices when we feel like we have done this too many times already. There are those out there that cannot afford to get the virus and there are those with other medical issues that need care that is being diverted towards resources for COVID-19.

Vaccines save lives, are safe, and prevent people getting sick enough to be in the hospital or in the ICU. There are some exceptions to these rules but I see this first hand playing out every day regardless of what is on any news channel or political camp. I don't watch news stations. What I see is real life not virtual. Additionally, masking indoors can make a difference when we are all consistent despite our extreme fatigue from doing this for 2 years.

As for real reasons that we will get through is our friends and family. Yes, in the last week it has been tough and I have felt it, but when that happens, people have shown up. They check in. In turn, we do the same for others. That is how we break this cycle when we take a closer look.

This holiday season, be present even when not physically there and please listen to one another. Pick up the phone or Facetime when you sense someone needs a call. If you are going to get together, consider testing beforehand to cut the risk. If you are struggling with mental health, please reach out to your doctors or professionals for help as you are not alone.

May everyone be safe, healthy, and well during these times. May we all find some peace."

I have been focusing my meditations on peace, comfort and ease often times using the guided Meta Meditation from David Hamilton. At the end of the meditation he offers, "And let's send this one out to all sentient Beings. May all sentient Beings be happy. May all sentient Beings be well. May all sentient Beings be safe. May all sentient Beings be at ease." At the end of the meditation he states, "Whatever you do today. Go well and go kindly."

On Friday night I looked out of our window and saw the almost full moon. Before I fell asleep, this poem flowed out of me:

Under the Moon

We are all One
under the light of the full moon
wintry barren branches frame its beauty

She beams inviting us to look up

Divisions must cease
who is right or wrong
transform these wayward passions

Come with compassion

In darkness and silence Source reigns
reign in conflicts
listen closely to heart's promptings

Prompting us to be light

Not right
foolishly clinging
digging in

Reach out

Building bridges
a time to heal
judgments fade into the fog
truth comes into view

A world made whole and new
Under the full moon
Where we are all One.

As the year comes to an end, I will focus on gratitude, healing, possibilities, HOPE, joy, love and peace. I will cherish the moments with loved ones and celebrate my 68th birthday with gusto. I will focus on Unity knowing that underneath it all we have so much more in common than what divides us.

From my heart to yours, with tidings of comfort and joy as we bring our lights to emerge from the darkness.

"Hope is the light. Trusted guide in darkness." ~Debasish Mridha

I wrote this poem on Christmas Eve as I prepared to celebrate my 68th birthday. I hope it inspires you as you embrace new beginnings in your life.

A New Chapter

Dipping my quill
poised to write a new chapter of my life
surrender to Source
troubles become light as a feather
fear fades
quivering quiets.

Creating
happily ever in present moment
my presence a gift to the world
heart and soul overflow with grace
gratitude for blessings
feeling blessings on their way.

Chapters of days gone by
reveal beauty and strength
stronger in broken places
gold gilding
healed and whole.

Infinite possibilities on a blank page
pure and powerful
Love reigns supreme
Love story for the ages
tethered to Source
lightness and ease
giddy with delight
exhilaration and excitement
ready.....set....go!

"Hope is the thing with feathers that perches in the soul - and sings without the words - and never stops at all." ~Emily Dickinson

resilience - {re-zil-ee-uhns} noun - English
the capacity of a person to maintain their core purpose and integrity in the face of dramatically changed circumstances, the ability to not only overcome setbacks but to also move forward.

On Monday, December 20, Broadway World announced that, because of the toll that the pandemic was taking on cast and company, "Jagged Little Pill" would be ending its Broadway run. I reached out to my Voices of Hope Boston family and we shared in the heartbreak while also sharing in a sense of hope that, as Greg Chastain said, "Talent always lands on its feet."

As I thought about what to write after Jagged closed, my theme was going to focus on how we have all learned through the pandemic to seize the day. I was going to wait until 'things got better' to go see Jagged next Spring and I am so grateful that I followed Spirit's promptings to go with Voices of Hope in November. There would not have been a show to see in the Spring. I've learned to generate more compassion and kindness in my interactions with my family and friends, keeping in check seeing people and situations through the lens of judgment. We never know when something might end.

Kathryn Gallagher who played Bella Fox in Jagged, was a guest on Stars in the House. She shared how her face reflected that she had been crying all day after receiving the news that her last performance was on December 17th. The show had closed for a few days due to the high rate of positive COVID-19 tests and made the painful decision to not reopen. During the interview she shared how she had a sense that the show might close. During what came to be her last performance, she said she thought about what if this would be her last show. She took in every moment and looked at every seat in the audience. While she shared how she and the members of the company were heartbroken, one could sense her strength through the pangs of grief. Her resilience was palpable throughout the interview. While once again feeling the sense of loss and uncertainty as a pandemic variant sweeps across the globe, I hold onto hope and light. After all, it IS Christmas - a time for hope, love, light and miracles.

Sean Allan Krill posted on Facebook:

Got to see my dear friend Kathy Voytko go on as Marian in The Music Man on Broadway tonight, and she was absolutely incredible. With virtually no rehearsal, she never missed a beat, never made a false move, looked, sang, and danced like a dream, made me laugh and broke my heart. She's a STAR. The real deal. And so is the show. The whole evening gave me hope in a very difficult, challenging time. And, okay, let's hear it for swings, understudies & standbys, for cry-eye! They are kicking ass and keeping Broadway up and running right now.
PS Hugh Jackman was a dream in the show as well, and gave the sweetest, heartfelt curtain speech about Kathy, and all the swings on tonight.

Despite his own heartache, he went out to support his dear friend and support the theater community that pulses through every cell of his body.

I receive emails from Broadway World as part of maintaining my connection to my New York roots and especially during the pandemic to keep up with the news from Broadway. When I started writing "Into the Light," I thought by now we'd be celebrating the robust return of shows and events during the holiday season. I never imagined that there would be news of friends' parents in the hospital during Christmas with COVID-19 or that shows would be closing. In the midst of it all there is light, hope, strength and remarkable resilience.

Broadway World shared a video and the transcript of what Hugh Jackman said during the curtain call at last night's show:

Hugh Jackman paid tribute last night to the "bedrock of Broadway" - understudies and swings while bringing forward Kathy Voytko who filled in for Sutton Foster on Thursday night in the Broadway show in a curtain call video captured on Instagram by Katherine Winter. Hugh told the audience "Kathy, when she turned up at work at 12 o'clock could have played any of 8 roles. It happened to be the leading lady. She found out at 12 noon today and at 1 o'clock she had her very first rehearsal as Marion Paroo. This is unprecedented. It's not only happening here at the Winter Garden...but all over Broadway. This is a time we've never known. We're in our 4th preview and we're all still learning, so swings and understudies have not had a chance to learn. They've watched from the corner of the room while we rehearse; while we get to practice over and over again. They just get to watch and write notes and then 5 hours before a performance they're told, you're on. All of these people here - the swings, and I'm emotional because it humbles me. The courage, the brilliance, the dedication, the talent. The swings, the understudies, they are the bedrock of Broadway."

The arts, especially musical theater are the bedrock of our lives. They take us through the entire range of human emotions and have the power to transform us. The collective experience of live theater bonds strangers together as time and space suspend during the performance. Musical theater has the power to make us laugh and cry and be in a state of awe immersing ourselves in another world.

If we look at what's happening right now, it would be easy to get drawn into the vortex of darkened theaters with shows and events cancelled due to the pandemic. But there is always a ghost light that stays on. That ghost light is our beacon of hope and resilience. We have vaccines, strength, resilience, faith and protocols to manage this phase of the pandemic. We have love to uphold us and heal us. We know we can do this. The show must go on!

Be Relentless! On Cake, Calamities and Compassion
December 28, 2021

"Compassion is not just feeling with someone, but seeking to change the situation. Frequently people think compassion and love are merely sentimental. No! They are very demanding. If you are going to be compassionate, be prepared for action!" ~Desmond Tutu

Last Monday I was planning to participate in David Hamilton's Personal Development Club Monthly Live Q & A. I got out for my run later than I had planned to because I wanted the day to warm up a bit. When I got home I debated about whether or not to attend the Zoom meeting since it was after the starting time and I needed to eat lunch. Yet something tugged at my soul to log on. I came in the middle of David sharing a part of his journey talking about listening to our intuition.

Someone posted a question privately to David. "I am doing meditations. I've let go of relationships that no longer serve me. I'm doing all the right things with nutrition and hydration but it's so hard to deal with the negativity and divisiveness that's going on in the world. Do you have any suggestions?"

David replied in his signature Scottish accent, *"I focus on being relentless with loving kindness and compassion. I do a meta meditation several times a day. When we do this meditation wishing well for ourselves and others not only are we sending out good energy into the world but we are changing our own chemistry so that it becomes easier to see the positive things in our lives and in the world."*

A woman asked a question in the chat about how to manage chronic pain due to arthritis. I had the opportunity to share with her my journey and healing resources as David talked about his recommendations for healing and management of chronic pain. I went on to share my journey with compassion saying how easy it is to feel hopeless and helpless when we are in pain but when we share healing stories, they uplift and inspire us.

So much compassion, love and kindness flowed among the members gathered that transcended being in cyberspace. As David teaches, consciousness transcends location and we can experience the flow of beautiful energy through our hearts as we express gratitude and compassion. Tears overflowed from our hearts as we wished everyone a happy Christmas and New Year.

Fast forward to Christmas Eve. Tom went to pick up my birthday cake. When he got home and we opened the box, we saw one of the ugliest cakes we had ever seen with writing that went around and down the side of the cake. At first I was angry and then I cried. I wanted Tom to take it back but then I took a pause. What if the regular cake decorator was out ill or they were short-staffed during the holidays. We have bought other cakes from this store before and they were never like this. Tom and Ruth Anne said they would go to another store and find a birthday cake for me. They were in short supply but they found one cake that they thought would be suitable and asked the person behind the counter if he could write on it. He proudly said of course he could. Tom and Ruth Anne picked up a small vegan chocolate cake that we have enjoyed before as a 'back up.'

They did not have the heart to say anything to the young man and when they brought the cake home I did not know whether to laugh or cry. He used a baby blue gel to write Happy Birthday Mary. He was clearly not a cake decorator nor someone who was able to properly write on a birthday cake. Tom and Ruth Anne said that it didn't look 'that bad' under the store's lighting. The small vegan chocolate cake would do just fine to celebrate my birthday.

When it came time to put the candles on the cake, they kept breaking because there was a hard chocolate shell rather than icing. We laughed so hard as the cake crumbled a bit until they found a festive red candle to put on the cake.

It was perfect for Tom, Ruth Anne, brother Autumn and partner Michelle via the Signal app to serenade me with Happy Birthday on Christmas.

While we could have focused on the cake calamities and certainly could have taken the cake(s) back to the managers with our complaints, we focused instead on the joy of celebrating Christmas and my 68th birthday. How wonderful it felt to greet the calamities with gratitude and compassion hoping that the young man at the bakery counter felt he made somebody's day special with his light blue gel artistry.

"God's dream is that you and I and all of us will realize that we are family, that we are made for togetherness, for goodness, and for compassion."

"Bringing people together is what I call 'ubuntu' which means I am because we are.' Far too often people think of themselves as just individuals, separated from one another, whereas you are connected and what you do affects the whole world. When you do well, it spreads out; it is for the whole of humanity." ~Archbishop Desmond Tutu

Desmond Tutu made his transition on December 26th. May we all be inspired to live his legacy especially during these times when we need to find our way back to healing and unity.

"And suddenly you just know it's time to start something new and trust the magic of beginnings." ~Anonymous

Many people often ask me what it's like to have a Christmas birthday. I grew up as Jewish so the only frustrating part was that my parents didn't want my brother to feel left out on Christmas so he received presents as well. I always had the day off from school and/or work. I had to celebrate my birthday before the holiday because friends had to spend time with family but we had great family celebrations at my cousins' house in the Bronx. Once I converted to Catholicism during my graduate education at the Boston College Graduate School of Social Work, it became very special for me to celebrate my Christmas Birthday. My husband's family invited us to join them on Cape Cod and the twins enjoyed raising a ruckus with all of their cousins.

Having a birthday that coincides with a beautiful religious holiday and the end of the year creates a wonderful time for contemplation and reflection. As the winter solstice approaches, neighborhoods are splendid with holiday lights and the anticipation of Christmas is in the air. Once Christmas arrives, the winter solstice has come and gone and we emerge into more light every day.

I am overcome by gratitude for all of the experiences of this past year. I am deeply grateful that we have all been healthy. Team McManus worked hard this year to let go of people and habits that were not healthy for us, allowed new people and experiences flow into our lives and been blessed to reconnect with friends through Ruth Anne's Providence Marathon run for Victory Programs.

As I begin another year and as we all get ready to embrace a new year, I open my heart to the magic of new beginnings. I am excited for new adventures in my work as a writer, poet and motivational speaker. I cherish being support crew for Ruth Anne and Tom on the road to Providence. I am hopeful we will be able to experience race-cations again in Providence and Cape Cod.

I plan to continue to work on releasing worries and fears, trusting that the Universe always has my back, making sure I set aside time every day to read books and get off screens, and have laser focus about what I want to co-create with Source in my life. This message popped up in my Facebook newsfeed. A message straight from the Divine.

December 30, 2021
Perspective of the Day

Start a new chapter.
Without dragging the old energy, the old dramas, and the old worries. Leave them in the past. Reignite your soul with fresh and healthy vibes.
You've come too far to let the old habits affect your journey. Greater things are coming your way and your heart needs to be open and free to receive them. You don't know how beautifully your story will unravel.
Trust & Believe
from Higher Perspective

It's time to relax, enjoy and trust the magic of new beginnings as Ruth Anne begins a new semester at Boston College, Tom begins a new contract job and I explore possibilities for sharing my gifts and journey as we say goodbye to 2021 and hello to 2022.

"Once upon a time...
She chose sneakers over heels.
She chose training over the chariot.
She chose the medal over her tiara
and
She ran like it was midnight." ~Anonymous

Last Saturday it was a sheet of ice on the ground, and we changed up our strength training day for a running day with Sunday. That meant I got out Tuesday and Wednesday for my 5K's.

On Tuesday, Tom and Ruth Anne had their 3 mile training run around the neighborhood. We started out together for their warm up and they went on their way training for Providence. I was able to enjoy the sights around the neighborhood on an unseasonably warm late December day. One of my favorite sights to capture was the raindrops gently hugging on to the berries glistening in the sunlight. I savored seeing green grass at the end of December.

On Wednesday I capped off my miles for 2021. Many of my runner friends run over 1,000 miles for the year so I am often shy to post my miles for the year at just over 500. But then I reflected on what an amazing accomplishment that is for this most unlikely runner and posted on Facebook, "With today's 3.25 miles, 2021 miles are done. Tomorrow and Friday are my rest days.

505 miles for the year ALL OUTDOORS which for many may not seem like a lot but 15 years ago I was given the prognosis of preparing to spend the rest of my life in a wheelchair. I celebrate every footstep and every mile I enjoy. While I am not racing these days, I am incredibly proud of my consistent health and wellness regimen."

2022 here we come with my goal of feeling gratitude for all my body gives me every day and for the gift of health and well-being!

To an amazing 2022 of miles filled with smiles!

I am excited to continue to motivate and inspire others with my powerful message of healing, hope and infinite possibilities. There are exciting projects that will take root and bloom in 2022. I have a commitment to daily affirmations from Louise Hay with her calendar and Power Thought cards. I am fierce to protect my time for meditation and reading every day and continue my dedication to my health and wellness journey.

To a year of resilience, gratitude, healing, strength, hope, joy, loving kindness and abundance for all Beings everywhere.

To finding the beauty in all things every day!

Since 2020 and all of my life experiences, I know that I have the resilience and strength to navigate these uncharted waters and be a beacon of light and hope in the darkness. So do you!

"Hope is a light in your heart that gives courage today and strength tomorrow." ~Anonymous

It was a dreary grey day in Boston yesterday. It was also a dreary day in the news which I briefly glimpse in the morning to stay informed of latest guidelines and guidance with the pandemic. Tom and Ruth Anne had a 3 mile speed drill workout to do as part of their marathon training program. I had my Monday morning 5K to run. When we do a neighborhood run, we are able to high five each other as we pass each other, each of us running at our own pace.

I thought to myself, "other than photograph Tom and RA for their photo album on the road to Providence what is there to take a picture of?" And then it hit me..."I need to take a picture of hope. A bare patch of ground that next Spring will blossom with flowers." I made a mental note to do that before I finished my run.

A short while later, I found a nickel! I smiled. "Oooh the Universe is giving me a high five!" And then I thought again. The movie, "The Five Pennies" chronicled bandleader "Red" Nichols journey with his daughter who contracted polio. Danny Kaye played Red Nichols. The movie came out in June 1959 when I contracted polio. It's a real tear jerker but speaks to strength and resilience. I got goosebumps to think that five pennies equals a nickel. The band was called The Five Pennies because "Red's" last name was Nichols!

Tom and Ruth Anne were on their cool down while I finished my run.

"Stop. I have to take a picture."

"Of what?" they asked. "Where you found the nickel?"

"No... of hope."

In just a few short months, despite all appearances to the contrary right now, beautiful flowers will poke their heads and move on to blossom throughout the Spring and Summer. There I was out on a run on a very cold day, 15 years after the diagnosis of Post-Polio Syndrome filled with healing, hope and infinite possibilities. I received a beautiful sign from the Universe while allowing hope to radiate from my heart.

"If you wait for perfect conditions you'll never get anything done."
~Anonymous

"It's only cold if you're standing still." ~Anonymous

When you read the title of this essay, you might have thought I'd be talking about how, during the pandemic, sweat pants became the outfit of choice. Between so many putting on weight and conducting business via Zoom and having nowhere to go, sweat pants became the fashion statement of the pandemic. But read on...

After Saturday's morning meditation, I checked my weather app. Did my eyes deceive me? Nope - it was 19 degrees Fahrenheit outside. The streets were relatively clear. Oh how I wanted to just hop on the treadmill and get in my 5K but Ruth Anne and Tom are training for the Providence Marathon and I knew they had to get outside for their 8 miles. Truth be told, I didn't feel like getting in miles after I made the mistake of doing a cursory check of the news headlines. I have opted to unsubscribe to the Boston Globe in my inbox. I cleared my energy and kicked my own behind out the door with a fresh mindset.

We had prepped our clothes the night before. We opened the door to get into the mindset of embracing the cold and psyching ourselves up to get in the miles despite the weather. Fortunately, the sun was shining. We debated about whether to do the Carriage Road on Heartbreak Hill or a neighborhood run. Since Tom and Ruth Anne had 8 miles, we opted for the Carriage Road and I would be support crew.

We were spoiled by moderate temperatures and dry ground until now.

We had our hearty pre-run breakfast, loaded up the car with provisions that included a book for me to read while waiting for Tom and Ruth Anne to finish their run and post-run fueling bananas.

Tom, Ruth Anne and I warm up together and they go off at their pace. There I was left to navigate the slush, snow and ice on the Newton Hills. One of the thoughts I have had to overcome is the programming I received after the diagnosis of Post-Polio Syndrome; "You have to be extremely careful if you are going to go out in winter. You should use a cane with an ice gripper and avoid falls for you are at high risk for a fracture." I straightened my spine and struck a power pose infusing myself with confidence. There were other runners on the Hills training for Boston. I fired up my mirror neurons reminding myself that while I may be slower than other runners, I am a runner, healed, healthy and strong. I've got this!

It was a cold, challenging run as runs after a snowstorm often are and I had to come up with an image that was going to help me get through.

"Sweat pants!" I thought about how great I was going to feel once I was back in the house changed out of my layers of running clothes and into my sweat pants. I transcended the challenge and discomfort of the moment by imagining how accomplished I would feel having conquered the Hills and the conditions. I also looked for the beauty in my run.

How blessed to see a heart in the snow, a bright blue sky and orbs letting me know that I was not running alone but Source's presence was with me every step of the way; as the Divine has been with me whenever I faced challenges in my life. Source has also been with me to fill my heart with joy and gratitude to celebrate magical moments.

Even though I turned around at the halfway point of 1.55 miles, my total miles were 3.2. I stretched when I got to the car, turned on the heater and WERS Standing Room Only show on the radio while I warmed up enjoying my banana and water.

"Hey where are you?" Tom and Ruth Anne asked in a text.

"I'm at the car and you?"

"We're heading there now and then we will have another two miles."

"Great. See you soon!"

We felt exhilarated for what we accomplished in less than optimal conditions. The big question after our Saturday run is, "What's for lunch?"

While Tom whipped up breakfast for lunch, I changed into my sweat pants. The comfort and relief was even more than what I imagined while navigating the hills. We savored every well-deserved bite and after our food was digested, we settled into a deep meditation with Jamie purring by my side.

Perspective: There are two ways to live your life - one is as though nothing is a miracle, the other is as though everything is a miracle. ~Albert Einstein

"Through the eyes of gratitude, everything is a miracle." ~Mary Davis

After Saturday's run, I was so grateful to wake up to melting snow and dry ground on Monday morning. As I did my 5K through the neighborhood while Tom and Ruth Anne did their 3 mile tempo run, I felt inspired to pick up my pace while feeling blessed by the glorious sunshine. Sunday was a dreary grey day in Boston and Monday's sunshine provided a delicious contrast to the gloom that dominated Sunday's skies.

Despite all the doom and gloom in the headlines, I felt uplifted with the sunbeams feeling my connection to the Divine in all of her glory. I reflected on the miracle of my healing from the effects of paralytic polio and trauma and the miracle of having overcome the diagnosis of Post-Polio Syndrome, which was due in large part to the unhealed trauma of my youth. We went out over Tom's lunch hour. We all devoured our lunch savoring not only the food but how great it feels to move our bodies outdoors in the winter.

Wednesdays are rest days for Tom and Ruth Anne so it's up to me to get my motivation gears in motion and get out the door to do my 5K. Temperatures were still in the teens when we got up, but the forecast called for moderating temperatures. By 11:30 the temperature went up to 36 degrees! Talk about perspective thinking temperatures were UP to 36 degrees Fahrenheit. I was ecstatic the arctic blast of minus 10 degrees with wind chill had quickly moved through. We've had winters when we've been 'trapped' in the Polar Vortex.

Ruth Anne insisted on taking a photo of me since I am the one who has been documenting their Providence Marathon run. Gratitude filled my heart that she wanted to acknowledge what I continue to accomplish in my own way at my own pace. I let the sun's warmth bathe me mind, body and soul reflecting on the miracle of healing in my life. Since we are in the middle of winter here in New England with barren trees and ground in New England, I looked to the skies for beauty. I captured the presence of the Divine and angels through my iPhone's camera's lens. I often use the hashtag every step is a gift and every mile is a blessing. I felt it with every footstep on Monday's and Wednesday's runs. I was running what could have been a boring and mundane run around the neighborhood. Instead the run was transformed by the attitude I chose to bring to the run.

I feel inspired by Tom and Ruth Anne's dedication, consistency and persistence with their training on the road to the Providence Marathon for Victory Programs and ReVision Urban Farm. Despite the climate of fear and uncertainty that dominates the headlines these days, people are incredibly generous with donations and words of support and encouragement. They know the marathon of healing that Ruth Anne endured and they know the integrity and passion that fuels Team McManus' journey on and off of the roads. The work that Victory Programs does saves lives and transforms lives. Their staff is second to none.

It could be so easy to get swept away once more, as we did in 2020, by the tsunami of divisiveness, terror, panic and hopelessness yearning for the pandemic to end. During these challenging times I find it is vital for our family and me to stay focused on goodness, doing good, feeling well, being well and, continue being unrelenting with compassion and kindness.

An attitude of gratitude and keeping perspective in my corner of the Universe sends out ripples of positive energy, love and moves the world into the light.

"The temps may drop but the running won't stop." ~Anonymous

We woke up to 11 degrees on Sunday morning but at least the wind chill below zero temperatures had passed. Tom and Ruth Anne had to get in their long run and I had to get in my 5K. It would have been easy for me to put on the space heater in our basement and fire up the treadmill but if they were going to brave the temps for 11-12 miles, so would I.

Once more, we carefully laid out our layers only this time, we had neck gators, two pairs of gloves and extra layers under and over the clothes we wore when it was 19 degrees since the air had gotten really cold overnight.

We pumped each other up to get out the door and did our "Gooo Team! We've got this!"

We 'warmed up' with a neighborhood run and planned to go around the small Reservoir but the icy patches made it too treacherous to stay there. Tom and Ruth Anne peeled off to go to Jamaica Pond and I made my way back to the neighborhood where there was dry ground. Even though my fingers felt frozen, I took off my glove to take a photo to capture the beauty of the winter day.

I used a technique I used when we trained for the 2009 Boston Marathon sending warmth to my extremities imagining warm lava flowing through me. My fingers and toes thawed and I settled into enjoying my run as the sun slowly warmed up the day. While I was running through the neighborhood a thought came to me comparing where I am today with where I was in December of 2006. One of the 'hallmark' symptoms of Post-Polio Syndrome is cold intolerance. The initial polio virus affected my body's thermostat; the ability to regulate my body temperature. I would shiver uncontrollably in the cold and profusely sweat in summer. But once I harnessed the power of the mind/body connection, I was able to fix my thermostat. I trained through the brutal New England winter experiencing all of its

219

beauty {and challenges} like I had never known before. I was told that I should use a cane with an ice gripper because one fall could result in a fracture that would lead to rapid decline in functioning. I did have several falls while running (none in winter) and aside from a bruised ego and scrapes on hands, knees and lip, I emerged victorious without a fracture.

While training for Boston, I wrote the poem Courage, inspired by a long run around Jamaica Pond on a bitter cold day:

Courage from "Feel the Heal: An Anthology of Poems to Heal Your Life"

The fear of ice and snow and slush embedded in my soul
a training run in winter - the path to Being whole.
A winter scene - Jamaica Pond - a feast for eyes' delight
to witness nature's splendor and behold this glorious sight.

A leaf - a tiny dancer - skating free without a sound
God's breath directs her movements
as She guides her twirling 'round.
Families of ducks decide to walk or take a dip
a comedy of errors into icy water slip.

Branches now bejeweled though bare bend with loving Grace
sparkling diamonds' anchor water's surface hold in place.
God's hand a glove of glistening snow hugs rocks along the wall
their heads peek out reminding me I'm answering God's call.

A scene I'd never witness if I let my fear take hold
courage triumphed, steppin' out with footsteps sure and bold.
Knowing that the pain subsides and Spirit can prevail
the Marathon is beckoning - through those miles I shall sail.

I celebrated the miles with Tom and Ruth Anne cheering them on via text as they dared to brave the elements for their long run. We marveled at how many runners were out on the roads on Sunday realizing that many opted to do their long run on the 'warmer' of the two weekend days. I felt exhilaration for my own run, celebrating the gift of health and wellness. I loved the thrill of being able to enjoy sunshine and blue skies despite cold temperatures. I recalled the exhilaration we felt during our Boston Marathon training after conquering the miles through the elements. Our longest run was 20 miles on a 17 degree day in March of 2009.

We were so fortunate that winter weather did not really begin until January this year. The sun is higher in the sky and it stays lighter after 4pm. I remember one winter when we were in the Polar Vortex. We had to keep our faucets dripping to make sure the pipes didn't freeze. I stay focused on the positive whenever possible and it's always possible.

After the first coldest run of the season a momentum begins that will now carry us through until Spring. There's a sense of exhilaration, resilience and strength that external circumstances do not dictate how we engage with life.

"Imagination is everything. It is the preview of life's coming attractions." ~Albert Einstein

During this morning's meditation, as the sun shined brightly through my bedroom window, I took deep breaths. Two feet of snow fell yesterday as the Blizzard of 2022 gripped the region. We bundled up and went out a couple of times to feel the refreshment of cold air and snow pelting our faces. Tom used our snow blower to dig us out. I hoped that the forecast for "feel likes below zero" temps would be wrong and that our street would be plowed and treated for us to be able to get out for a run.

Before checking my phone for weather, emails and social media posts, I did a Meta Meditation sending out well wishes for myself, my loved ones and all Sentient Beings everywhere. I felt Spirit's presence speak to me, "Feel as if it were Spring!" I felt my heart open and gratitude flood every cell of my Being. We made it through the storm. Electricity stayed on. There was absolutely no storm damage despite blizzard force winds and snow falling at times at 2-3 inches per hour.

I asked myself, 'How would I feel if I woke up to a beautiful Spring morning?'

As if on cue, Jamie meowed and came bounding onto our bed. She stretched with her whole body and I followed suit ready to greet the day.

After the diagnosis of Post-Polio Syndrome, I lived my life as if I were already healed. Despite all appearances to the contrary, and having been told to prepare to spend the rest of my life in a wheelchair, I imagined myself running, dancing, splashing in puddles, forgiving the past and being grateful for the gifts of the challenges I faced. With fierce determination, I worked in physical therapy and then a personal trainer to get to the finish line of the 2009 Boston Marathon and beyond. I learned the healing power of imagination, of writing poetry and the body's tremendous capacity to heal once I ignited the spark of my Spirit that was crying out for healing.

When the winter of our lives bears down, it is easy to forget that we have the power to choose how we feel whatever the weather and whatever our current circumstances may be. I imagine a time when we no longer wear masks and the headlines report the pandemic's end as they did with polio.

Although it feels like 2 degrees outside right now and black ice lines our street, I feel the warmth of the sun through the windows. I imagine seeing bare ground again and our tulips poking their heads through the garden once more. I see the buds on the trees and the leaves forming a canopy of love in the 'little field' across from our home. It always seems as though they magically and spontaneously burst into bloom yet we know there is a slow process of transformation.

I was in the deep dark winter of my life in December of 2006 and yet I found a way to imagine myself being in the Springtime of my life. I was 53 years old when I found my way to the sport of running. I wrote poetry and visualized my Boston Marathon run from taking those first steps as a newbie runner to how it would feel to cross the finish line on April 20 of 2009.

We are so blessed to be living at this time when research has done studies to prove the power of the imagination and its effects on the body. The mind and body cannot distinguish between what is in our imagination and what is real.

Despite the mounds of snow, the barren trees, the temps on my weather app all saying we are still in the depths of winter, my thoughts and feelings warm my heart and soul as if it were Spring.

Seasons

They're called seasons
for a reason
reminders of impermanence
mirroring ebb and flow of life
challenging us to find beauty in winter's barren trees
spying berry bush frosted with capping of snow
finding delight in rosy red cheeks
hot cocoa to warm body and soul.

Miracle of buds herald Spring's arrival
teasing us with winter's end
no season lasts forever!

As colors burst forth layers shed
anticipation of carefree summer days
savoring sensations
sun's warmth melts away winter's woes
deep breaths of summer's sweetness
yearning for time to stand still
basking in glorious sunsets of a late evening stroll.

As days shorten once more
vibrant greens begin to pale
opportunity for rebirth in Autumn's splendor
resilience realized
harvesting Hope in transformation
rising to embrace all the seasons of my life.

"How many lessons of faith and beauty we should lose, if there were no winter in our year." ~Thomas Wentworth Higginson

Last Thursday the temperatures climbed into the 40's. We watched the piles of snow from the Blizzard of 2022 begin to dwindle. There was bare pavement and even though the day was grey and cloudy, I felt the stirrings of Spring in my heart as my heart tuned into a few birds singing their song. When I saw the forecast for Friday I thought, "This can't be happening. They must be getting it wrong."

There was a Winter Weather Watch that turned into a Winter Weather Advisory with flash freezing. Friday morning brought lots of rain and we thought, "Yup they missed the forecast." We went about our day. The social media feed filled with car accidents and a flash freeze happening across the region. The rain turned to sleet and covered sidewalks, bushes and cars.

I was in awe of how quickly it happened.

Having yet another Friday storm begged the question of whether or not we would be able to get out for our Saturday morning run. Tom and Ruth Anne had a half marathon scheduled on their training plan. I am not one to experience cabin fever but as the sleet rained down (pun intended) I felt agitated. I knew I had no control over the weather and the ice that quickly gripped the region so I knew I had to get a grip on myself! I meditated and surrendered to what was happening. Fortunately Tom was able to safely get our groceries. We hoped that our Town would do a good job at making our neighborhood safe for our Saturday run.

I felt deep in my soul that we just had to get out for our Saturday run. Nine miles on the treadmill for Ruth Anne last Sunday followed by two days of running in the cold caused her knee to become injured. Fortunately, on Wednesday, she had an appointment with her acupuncturist who specializes in the treatment of sports injuries.

He is also a physical therapy assistant and personal trainer. He uses a combination of sports acupuncture, manipulative therapy and KT tape to facilitate recovery. Tom had dug us out from the Blizzard of 2022 and had done a 10K on the treadmill. His back and legs were very sore. We knew there was no way we would do another treadmill run. My knees were not happy with my treadmill 5K.

As the official Marathon Manager for Tom and Ruth Anne, I got everything ready for their Half Marathon; their longest run in this training cycle. They both thought I was crazy to go ahead as if we were going to be able to get out and get in a run but I know the power of intention. We woke up to freezing temperatures but glorious sunshine streaming through our windows. It was hard to tell whether or not the streets were safe to run. We debated about whether or not we would get in our run and if the answer were yes, where we would go. As I looked out the window, a runner passed by. "It's a sign," I yelled upstairs to Tom and Ruth Anne who were getting dressed.

I filled up the water bottles and set up the 'aid station' on the dining room table. We donned our layers and did a "Gooo Team" before heading out the door. The first few moments were testy as we all worked to find our footing. Ruth Anne wanted to abort the mission but I pointed out, "We have no choice. It's too late to head over to try to find another route. We can't do the treadmill especially for a Half Marathon for you and Tom. There's lots of bare ground. It's time for a mental toughness run."

When we crossed paths during our loops, I was going to suggest that they might think about a run/walk strategy given the conditions. I saw them walking and they shared that they decided on that strategy after their first few miles!

The warmth of the sun was delicious despite the cold air.

I could feel the Divine with us in every step.

I felt triumphant after my 5K and experienced the excitement and anticipation of Tom and Ruth Anne doing their longest run for this training cycle. I rang my cowbell as they completed their 21 loops on Eliot Street for 13.1 miles!

As we celebrated with pizza and tuna subs we reminisced about our Boston Marathon training. Twenty one loops around the neighborhood was sure better than 117 laps around the BU track. We reminisced about our first half marathon as Team McManus in Hyannis in February of 2009. Even though we won't be a part of Hyannis this year, I felt a deep sense of joy and exhilaration rise up within me remembering those magical moments of my first Half Marathon.

There is so much we are yet unable to experience during COVID-19 but not having access to a gym is a blessing. We have no choice but to go outside, brave the elements and experience the sense of power that comes with embracing the elements. The weather has been frightful these past two weeks, challenging the mettle of even the heartiest New England residents. As runners, we are trained to be strong, resilient and harness the power of our mental toughness to not let frightful weather makes our lives miserable.

As often happens in February, we see temperatures slowly on the rise and the snow piles melt. What a treat to see 57 degrees with sunshine in the forecast for Saturday.

When the weather outside is frightful I always remember, no storms last forever. Spring always returns. Resilience and strength prevail when we call on those qualities from deep within our heart and soul.

After the Storms

Blizzard and ice storms
sub-zero temperatures
seemingly never ending winter
housebound
grey and gloom
thoughts turn to doom
What if's swirl with bone chilling winds.

Does any storm last forever?

Sun returns
greets me with a warm hug
stepping outside door's threshold
having met my threshold
temporarily lost my way
even in the midst of winter storms
though invisible to the eye
Divine's presence shines brightly
always guiding us home
into the light.

A Word About Wordle   February 18, 2022

How did this simple word game worm its way into our lives and social media? When I first saw people posting about Wordle, I told myself that I would stay as far away from it as I could without success. Being fascinated with words, language, puzzles and games, I was easily drawn into its daily mystique of an empty board of 6 rows and 5 columns. During breakfast, I ponder what word I am going to use to start my Wordle of the Day.

One of my friends posted on Facebook that you can also do the Archived Wordles if you were late to the party as I was. It's become a morning and evening ritual that brings a mix of joy, frustration, curiosity and, according to many articles, is really good for our brain health. There was one extremely challenging Wordle that I let sit for awhile as I went about my day. I saw a "Yield" sign and the next thing I knew, the answer just came to me. When I got home, I entered the letters and they all turned green.

An article in The Washington Post, "What Our Brains Do When We Play Wordle," gave a brief overview of the history of Wordle and why it has become our new drug. The article was written by a Tufts University psychologist. It's comforting to know that our obsession with Wordle is good for our cognitive health.

Wordle seems to be another 'silver lining' of the pandemic. I'm not sure it would be as popular if we were all leading our pre-pandemic lives not having as much time at home or spending as much time connecting with each other on social media. It's a fun way to check in with friends and family. It's a great conversation starter as we share our results. It's something tangible, constant and a part of new rituals. We celebrate each other's triumphs and tribulations. At first blush it may seem trivial, but given how the pandemic had limited our lifestyles, having something novel to experience every day, and being able to share that experience with each other has boosted everyone's mood and brain health.

In one instance, Wordle saved the life of an 80 year old woman. She texted her Wordle results to her daughters every day. When they didn't receive the text and she didn't answer her phone, the daughters became quite concerned. They sent a neighbor to check on her. When her car was there but their mother didn't answer the door, they knew something was wrong. They called the police where their mother lived and they discovered she was being held hostage by an intruder who was suffering a mental health crisis.

Of course, as with anything that takes the internet by storm, there are those who criticize the Wordlers, (I think I just made up a new word) and say they don't get it. There are those who are disgruntled by what they perceive the NY Times did to Wordle when it bought the game. There are those who express their anger by revealing the word and you can Google Wordle word of the day and get the answer.

There are those who swear off Wordle only to be drawn back into its magical vortex. I enjoy when Wordle is trending on Twitter to see people posting the first time they lost the game with their funny memes or conversely the first time they solved the puzzle in two tries. It's often the same word that is the most challenging for most people and if a word that is challenging for me is easy for one of my friends or family members, I celebrate their ingenuity at being able to solve it in two or three tries. Strategies are shared and self-proclaimed geeks try to find an algorithm that will help them solve the puzzle. If I get stuck, I bring out old fashioned paper and pen to play with the letters. The intention of the creator of Wordle was to provide a distraction for his girlfriend during the pandemic. He has created so much more! I hope that Wordle will become a classic word game and that it keeps its simple once a day formula that brings people together with a five letter wordle of the day.

Postscript 7/18/2022: We now have Quordle, Octordle, Heardle, Waffle Game, Foodle, Framed and I'm sure many more iterations that I'm not aware of. What great fun we have sharing the latest versions of games based on Wordle's concept and who is willing to venture into a new realm of on line games. The conversations and connections continue with warmth and lighthearted play.

Rest and Hope - My Favorite Four Letter Words   February 26, 2022

Rest Days:
Restock glycogen stores
Build strength
Minimize fatigue
Reduce risk of overuse injuries
Avoid mental burnout
Help your body repair itself

For the past two years during the pandemic, I've been doing three 5K's a week, and two days of strength training. I missed getting into a pool but took great pride of the strength and well-being I experienced. Being outdoors whatever the weather, breathing in fresh air and experiencing sunshine during winter and running by the ocean in summer helped us to navigate the pandemic. Thursday and Friday were my rest days.

With Tom and Ruth Anne training for Providence, I wasn't taking two rest days together. I was doing my 5K's at 6am once a week, often times on slushy roads. I wasn't taking time to recover after my 5K runs because I was support crew for Tom and Ruth Anne. I forgot to "put on my own oxygen mask first." My runs were getting more sluggish and I experienced more joint pain and muscle spasms. I ignored the early signs of what was happening in my body having been so caught up in the thrill of Ruth Anne and Tom's journey on the Road to Providence to raise money and awareness for Victory Programs. I had also increased my strength training. I decided to curtail the increase in reps and weights hoping that adjustment would be all that was needed.

Two weeks ago my body said, "Okay. That's enough." There was no way I could continue to push myself. Fortunately I stopped before I experienced a major injury. I listened to the level of discomfort I experienced and made the necessary changes. I practiced more self-care including stretching using a strap, a ball to roll out my feet and my massage stick taking time out during the day to care for myself mind, body and soul. I intensified my meditation practice and once again harnessed the power of the mind/body connection to heal the inflammation, increase fluidity in my joints and return to a feeling of ease in my body. I know and trust my body's tremendous capacity to heal as I have worked with my body for the past 15 years to achieve what some would say are impossible goals and heal what some would say could only be healed with surgery, by harnessing the power of the mind/body connection.

I talked with Tom and Ruth Anne about the adjustments we needed to make to take some of the stress off of me while they trained and fundraised for Providence. I talked with myself about adjusting my response to their training and making sure that I was taking better care of myself. I reflected on how I was pushing myself especially with hills. Because of a preponderance of ice and snow, we had to run around our neighborhood. There is no way to avoid the incline that starts at the end of our street. I was getting tired of doing the same route over and over and over again. I took a turn up a hill we used when we trained for the 2009 Boston Marathon. File that under what was I thinking! I wasn't and it was after that run that I realized I had gone too far. I pushed myself through one more 5K after that run (old habits die hard) before realizing enough was enough for now.

I continued strength training incorporating a lot of stretching into the program. I gave myself permission to take time off from my 5K's. Starting tomorrow I will go back to basics and go out for a one mile walk while Tom and Ruth Anne get in their 15 miles. I'll see how I feel and figure out a plan from there. I had to silence what the medical community told me as a survivor of paralytic polio. Instead, I recalled this New York Times Op-Ed piece that the doctor who took care of me after I contracted polio wrote when I was doing research for my Trilogy of Transformation:

Caution and Hope On Polio 'Signs'
Published: March 3, 1985
I read with interest the article entitled "A Group for Polio Survivors Who Have New Symptoms" (Feb. 10).
Having supervised the rehabilitation of poliomyelitis patients at Grasslands Hospital during the epidemics of the 50's and 60's,

probably including the "then" infants mentioned in the article, I would like to add a word of caution and even hope as an afterthought.

Firstly, there is no reason to suspect deterioration in the nerve cells in the spinal cord. After 30 years, one must accept some loss of endurance, increased fatigue and even some discomfort induced by other unrelated medical problems. This is true in the athlete with repeated injuries, in the obese person with back problems and even in the jogger with foot ailments.

Any individual with paralytic disability in an extremity will experience the normal process of "wear and tear" except that it may be more difficult to adjust to it. Just as one learned to compensate for the initial impairment so must one adjust to the later, more subtle changes rather than develop an emotional hang up of being a "polio victim." ~Eugene Moskowitz, M.D. Mount Vernon

One of the things I kept hearing after receiving the diagnosis of Post-Polio Syndrome was "we don't want to give you false hope."

False hope? Is there really such a thing?

"Wishes are false. Hope is true. Hope makes its own magic." ~Lars Taylor

Unfortunately there are many in the medical community who believe there is such a thing as false hope and hope to many in Western Medicine is a four letter word. I could have easily succumbed to the diagnosis and prognosis I was given in December of 2006 but somehow I was able to muster the courage to do what I'd done ever since I was 5 years old. I opened myself to Divine Guidance and a touch of grace.

Instead of returning to the Post-Polio Clinic as I had after a knee injury in December of 2014, I turned to myself, the Divine and my loved ones to get back on track. I had to embody my healed self. Old trauma wounds surfaced and I embodied myself as the powerful, glorious woman I have become since the diagnosis of Post-Polio Syndrome. I had fleeting moments wondering if perhaps my body had MS or Parkinson's and reminded myself that the body achieves what the mind believes. I used Emile Coue's mantra of "Every day in every way I am better and better." I felt compassion and kindness for myself realizing that the symptoms I experienced were the perfect storm of two years of COVID-19, a reaction to the booster shot, the changes that came with Tom and Ruth Anne's marathon training, Tom starting a new contract job, Ruth Anne looking for a job, after her temporary job ended, and not paying attention to what my body was telling me. As is always true, it's not the stress itself that is important but how I choose to respond to it. Everything was weighing me down. I briefly became victim and martyr.

I am back on track with self-care, finding ease and grace in my body again, revisiting trauma wounds that needed deeper healing and continue to be in awe of what happens when I connect to Source. I have rediscovered my love for rest and hope. The seeds of healing are bearing fruit. I am excited to feel a wonderful blossoming of mind, body and soul as Spring moves into Boston. I am grateful to my body for the symptoms that led me back to Source and back to myself. We are coming up on the two year anniversary of when life came to a screeching halt with the pandemic of 2020. I've learned, and continue to learn soul lessons. Much trauma has come to the surface and while, on the one hand I felt frustrated that traumatic memories resurfaced, I realized that this has been a tremendous opportunity for healing on deeper levels. I am no stranger to having a total upheaval of life. Aah if only there were an easier way to experience growth and transformation.

Hyannis Marathon Weekend will go on next weekend. I feel twinges of sadness we will not be a part of it but I know in my heart it will be a shadow of its former self. The pre-race Pasta Dinner was cancelled on Friday. There was no Expo. Frank Shorter graciously agreed to be the guest at bib pick up on Saturday. There was a much smaller field of runners. One of my dear friends from what we affectionately called Camp Hyannis sent me a message asking if we were going to

Hyannis. "Will you be speaking again or running on Sunday? I will be walking the 10K." I told her I felt twinges of sadness when I saw the Facebook posts of the area that was traditionally filled with Expo vendors and was now designated for bib and t-shirt pick up. I reminded her (and myself) we hold so many great memories of our shared experiences during Hyannis Marathon Weekend. Its presence in 2022 seems to book end the pandemic.

The Massachusetts State House will reopen to the public after being closed for 700 days. Today's Boston Globe headline stated, "Mayor Wu Lifts Vaccine Mandate Immediately." There is still much confusion and disparities among towns and states about vaccine and mask mandates. There's a push to get a booster shot yet the question of whether or not being fully vaccinated would include getting a booster shot, is now on the back burner. All the metrics indicate that the 'surge' from omicron and delta variants has ended.

Despite the forecast of another February snow/ice storm, I felt this poem pour out of me

Can You Feel It?

Stepping outside my door
I feel it
anticipation of Spring
transported without plane, train or boat
breathing deeply
an elixir from earth ready to give birth
heart flutters with hope.
Infinite possibilities
emerge from winter's womb
ultimate faith seeing the unseen
confidence of beauty unfolding
doubt yields to faith
barren trees poised to pop
sun's warmth enticing transformation.

Eager to shed
letting go
Spring's renewal
enters soul
eternally grateful
it happens every year.

At the end of the Hyannis Marathon Weekend, Race Director Paulie posted this on Facebook:

February 28 at 3:00 PM ·
Have been loading up the van slowly and just taking in how long I have been doing Hyannis....how much the town has been part of my life...how many people have been part of this event and my life...I not so fondly remember the first year... Fred Kirk and Paul Clark were my roadies...we were all in our early and mid 30's.

The first year I didn't dare head back to the hotel because it wasn't my finest moment as a race director coupled with a blizzard at the start and there were some angry runners...yesterday I was at the podium all afternoon drinking beer with Frank Shorter perhaps the Greatest American Runner EVER and listening for hours as people told us how happy they were to be back in Hyannis and to be getting back some semblance of life that they knew...most don't realize how important these events are for many...many use them for their physical and mental well-being...for some it's their sole social mechanism....and financially it's a huge boost...Gary the bartender hadn't worked since December 2021 and yesterday was a huge boost for him....same for many of the conference staff here who had lost work due to so many events being canceled.

As for me...I came out of mi Madres womb saying "on yer mark, get set, GO" so yesterday was a needed release aka medication for me also. Hoping we will all be able to safely gather again in February of 2023.

Hugs, Hope and Smiles for Miles on Heartbreak Hill
March 13, 2022

"Hope is being able to see that there is light despite all the darkness." ~Desmond Tutu

"Should we just go out the front door today?" Tom asked as Team McManus prepared to get in their miles on a soggy Saturday.

"I desperately need a change of scenery," I said.

"All right then," Tom replied, "Let's do Heartbreak Hill."

As often happens when Team McManus is training for an endurance event, we squabble over the silliest things. As we got into the car, the rain picked up.

"See if we would have gotten out the door sooner," Ruth Anne proclaimed, "we would have missed the heaviest rains."

That's true but oh we would have missed out on so much more.

When I came out of my morning meditation, a little limerick was percolating knowing that the mask mandate ended in Brookline, one of the last cities and towns in Massachusetts to lift the mandate:

Today's the day the masks are gone our faces are happy and free
it's the end of the pandemic everyone's smiles we get to see.
There's now times for hugs galore two years almost to the day....

Little did I know the hugs galore I was about to experience.

We pulled into our regular spot in the parking lot before Centre Street and Commonwealth Avenue. We were getting our fuel belts together and a runner came toward us. "Well isn't this wonderful? Hello Mary McManus."

When he saw the puzzled look on my face he said, 'It's David O'Leary.'

"Oh my goodness," I replied. I immediately thought that if we would have gone out earlier we would have missed this opportunity to see him and so many others out on the course.

David is the host of Magic 106.7's Morning Magic radio show here in Boston. We've been friends for years.

We walked toward each other and he said, "Can I give you a hug?..." and as he said 'I'm fully vaccinated...' we were already hugging each other.

"Is this your beautiful family?"

I introduced him and asked if we could take a selfie together. He was out on his 18 miler running his 2nd Boston Marathon (the first one in October) for American Foundation for Suicide Prevention and was gracious enough to take a moment with us.

Tom, Ruth Anne and I set out for our miles. As part of their training for the Providence Half Marathon, they do a 10 minute warm up before they go off at their pace. As we crossed Centre Street, we saw a water stop in the distance wondering whose it was. There stood 1976 Boston Marathon Champion, Jack Fultz, our friend and coach for the Dana Farber Cancer Boston Marathon team. We hesitated for a moment before giving each other a hug. We chatted for a few moments with eyes smiling. Tom and Ruth Anne went on their way to get in their long run.

I am still in recovery mode getting back to running after needing time off. It was a short out and back for two miles. On my way back to our car I hear, 'Hi Mary!' It was Erin, Ruth Anne's Occupational Therapist from Spaulding running this year's Boston Marathon as part of the Race for Rehab Team. She was ready to run in 2020 but then COVID-19. She ran the Virtual Marathon in September but she wanted the experience of the in person Boston Marathon.

I asked her if she saw Ruth as she calls Ruth Anne.

"Yes back there."

"Have a great rest of your run," I said as she sped past me.

One of my favorite questions to hear while on Heartbreak Hill is from out of towners running their first Boston. "Is this Heartbreak Hill?" I heard a woman ask the other members of her group. Someone started to explain it to her so I knew I didn't need to stop to explain it to her. I smiled warmly to myself realizing that after two years, Boston will run again in April.

I passed the Dana Farber Charity Teams water stop.

"Great job," they said.

I smiled saying how I wasn't training for Boston.

"That doesn't matter. You're out here and you're doing a great job. Would you like some refreshment?" I thanked them and we shared in the gratitude and joy of feeling a sense of emerging from the pandemic.

As I was nearing the end of my run, I saw Erin in the distance. She was waiting for the light to change to cross the street to the Heartbreak Hill Running Company. We greeted each other in the pouring rain and hugged with our eyes. She had just finished her 20 miles. She told me what a total joy it is to see Ruth and her dad running together. I gave her a brief update and told her how she is with us every day. The seeds that she planted through her sessions with Ruth continue to blossom. I expressed my deepest gratitude to her and gestured by placing my hands over my heart. She is a gifted professional who continues to provide support through emails.

When I got back to the car I stretched. Amanda was about to run by me. I got to know Amanda through the Facebook running community. I loved her posts with her 'memere' who lived with dementia. Amanda shared her weekly visits with her on Facebook. The love they had for each other was palpable despite her advancing dementia. We smiled from our hearts as she said, "I saw them back there. They look great." {referencing Tom and Ruth Anne} I wished her a great rest of her run. When we got home we messaged each other on Facebook and made donations to each other's fundraisers. She is running with Team Camp Shriver. Since 2006, Camp Shriver at the University of Massachusetts Boston has welcomed children, ages 8-12, from low income families in the Boston area to a free inclusive summer recreational camp.

The rain and wind intensified but there was a sense of unbridled joy and gratitude in the runners' energy. It's counterinutitive to think that running on the hills would facilitate my healing but there was powerful medicine and magic on the Newton Hills on Saturday. As I got in and out of the car while waiting for Tom and Ruth Anne to finish their miles, I noticed how I was able to walk with greater ease and much less pain from just two weeks ago. Tom, Ruth Anne and I agreed it was the best we felt in two years!

They were literally soaked to the skin with hearts filled with joy and gratitude at the end of their run.

At a time when the world seems to be filled with worry and fear, divisiveness and feelings of lack, there were hugs, hope and smiles for miles on Heartbreak Hill as runners fundraise for important causes and as a community, Boston gets ready to run again!

It's beginning to look a lot like Christmas...

Wait? What did she just write? Christmas? It's March 23rd.

In Boston, we call Boston Marathon weekend Runners Christmas. For the past two years, this annual tradition was cancelled. It's been a part of my life since I ran the 2009 Boston Marathon as a mobility impaired runner defying the diagnosis of Post-Polio Syndrome. I've been blessed to become a part of the running community that grows exponentially every year as we meet friends of friends. I've often said that running friendships are like instant oatmeal - just add water or in this case - just add running and friendships are forged.

The hills have been alive with the energy of runners exhilarated that Boston runs again in April. The Facebook feed is filling with bib numbers and statements like "Can't wait to see you in April." I feel goosebumps just typing that phrase. One of our dear runner friends shared the photo of one of the banners for the 126th Boston Marathon celebrating 50 years of when women were first 'allowed' to run in the Boston Marathon.

It is exhilarating to begin planning meet ups with friends coming in from out of town and meet ups with friends from Boston who I haven't seen since the pandemic. There was a taste of the excitement of the Boston Marathon in October but it did not have the rite of Spring and the feel of Runners Christmas that the running of the Boston Marathon has in April.

Two years ago our City and the world was in a state of shock and fear, seeking ways to navigate life turned upside down. While trees were beginning to bloom and flowers poked through the once frozen ground, there was an eerie silence to Springtime in Boston. I began to write poetry again as a way to cope with the all-pervasive anxiety set against the backdrop of yellow caution tape on the silenced playgrounds and all but essential businesses closed. My pen became my divining rod for healing once more as it had after the diagnosis of Post-Polio Syndrome 15 years ago. I channeled messages of hope, healing, optimism and seeing a future that transcended the current circumstances at the time. Those poems and essays blossomed into "Hope is a Garden: Poems and Essays From the 2020 Pandemic."

Facebook reminded me today of all that I was grateful for a year ago:
I am so grateful and appreciative of:
Toilet paper
Upcoming appointments with my chiropractor after 14 months
A hair stylist appointment after 13 months
Children having fun on the playground
School in session
Hope for ending the pandemic with the vaccines
Economic relief for restaurants and small businesses
So many things we once took for granted that now we can appreciate in deeper ways.

Tom received his first vaccine on March 23rd last year.

Restaurants are buzzing with activity again and the whole city is coming alive in anticipation of Spring and the 126th running of the Boston Marathon. Runners have one more long run before they taper and count down to the first Boston Marathon Weekend in April in two years.

Boston Marathon weekend is a time when reunions happen and the magic of the Unicorn fills the air. As the daffodils line the Boston Marathon route, the City comes alive with blue and yellow colors. This year those colors take on even more significance as we pray for and support Ukraine. May the Spirit that fills our City during this time of year create ripples of joy, peace, strength, resilience, love, harmony and unity for the rest of our world.

Merry Runners Christmas!

Two Years Later

A future once imagined now within sight
emerging from pandemic into the light.
Springtime rebirthing sky brilliant blue
vibrant colors the signal that we made it through.
We held onto Hope in midst darkness and fear
Source abiding reminding take heart I'm right here.
Though winter's grip seemed to have us firm in its hold
we dared dream of a future no more shivering with cold.
Two years what a journey unmasked with hugs now we greet
navigated times of uncertainty excited for a time when we'd meet.
Eyes shimmering with tears grateful hearts overflow
manifesting health and well-being in pandemic's wake we now grow.
Times of uncertainty they are all part of life
but we'd never imagined such heartache and strife.
Clouds of despair now dispersing warm sunshine we live life anew
with steadfast faith and each other we made it through.

Facebook reminded me that today is the one year anniversary of when I received my first vaccine. The Boston Marathon returns in all its glory this weekend. The City is alive with anticipation as a symbol of 'normalcy' returns when Boston runs again on Monday.

Running, meditation and being part of David Hamilton's Personal Development Club along with continuing to write poems and essays helped me to focus on hope, optimism, faith, continued healing and growth throughout these past two years.

In last week's Personal Development Club, David gave us a booster shot of exercises to improve self-esteem and self-love. We are all experiencing pandemic weariness and that weariness can take a toll on one's capacity to stand tall as Divine Beings. It was exactly what I needed as we continue to emerge from the pandemic and return to experiencing our place in a world very different than the world we lived in before March of 2020. Harnessing the power of the mind/body connection which is bi-directional, David gave us exercises and a meditation/visualization to boost confidence. Our mind influences our body and in turn, our body can influence our thoughts and our feelings. He referenced Amy Cuddy's TED Talk about body language and his book, "I Heart Me."

I've been practicing my meditations/visualizations to embody strength and confidence and release fear and anxiety reminding myself how worthy I am to receive life's blessings. This poem was borne out of that time of visualization/meditation using the phrase that flowed through David during our session, "plant your feet in the soil of self-esteem".

Standing Tall

Feel the vibration of love
quaking in fear no more
tears water the garden of my soul
washing away past
planting feet in soil of self-esteem.
Roots deep
firm in faith
though winds may blow
I bend with ease and grace
I know my place as Divine
radiant Being.

Speaking my Truths
live and let live
others may turn a blind eye
no matter
weeding worries
bury seeds of judgement resentment
acceptance and forgiveness bloom.

Worthy to receive
joy in giving
Essence of who I am
essential to feeling free
a shift
from withering wall flower
unwavering
bathing in Truth of my existence
expecting miracles
I blossom and grow.

As one who experienced severe abuse as a child after contracting
paralytic polio, there are times when I need a booster shot of self-
love especially during these unprecedented times to go into the light,
be the light and feel light as we emerge from the pandemic.

"Boston is the cream of the crop of the marathon world. It has such history that you feel such honor just being a part of it." ~Summer Sanders

"As marathoners we know about pacing, about hard days, about broken dreams and yet we keep showing up. We hang onto hope. We can beat this current storm. We will win this race. And the after party will be glorious!" ~Anonymous

And what a glorious after party we had at the 126th running of the 2022 Boston Marathon on 4/18/2022. It had been 1,099 days since the tradition of the Boston Marathon, run on the 3rd Monday in April took place.

Ever since I ran the 2009 Boston Marathon, the tradition of all that is the Boston Marathon has been a part of our lives. In 2011, Tom ran Boston for Childrens Hospital. In 2013 we returned to the Mandarin and joined our Race for Rehab Team. Unfortunately the day did not end as a typical Marathon Monday but on the third Monday in April in 2014, Boston ran again and Meb won! We have our special spot to spectate on the corner of Dean Road and Beacon Street just before Mile 23. Except for 2018 as the rains and cold winds prevailed, we watched the race in person, tracking and cheering on our friends with signs and #morecowbell.

We knew that the energy would be unlike any we had known after a two year hiatus. The weather was spectacular. Tom and Ruth Anne had a shake-out training run scheduled as they prepare for their Providence Half Marathon on May 1st. We debated about whether or not to get our seats secured or if they should first do their run. We were wise to postpone their run as Beacon Street spectators were out bright and early.

We had a front row seat to see Daniel Romanchuk as the lead wheelchair.

We turned to the spectators around us and as if we were of one mind, marveled at how he had such an incredible lead. There was no other racer in sight. There was a six minute difference between 1st and 2nd place in the wheelchair division!

We were hoping to see American women lead the field but Olympian Molly Seidel had to leave the race at mile 15 due to a hip impingement. Nell Rojas once again took top American woman for the 2nd year in a row. She finished 10th overall for the women's race. Desi Linden always receives a roar of cheers from the crowd.

It was a thrilling fight to the finish for the top two women, Peres Jepchirchir and Ababel Yeshaneh, separated by only 4 seconds after Peres Jepchirchir broke the finisher's tape. We could see from our vantage point that it was a tight race as they raced and chased each other down Beacon Street.

We had a bit of a breather after the lead runners passed through before the real challenge of the day began; finding our runner friends among the throngs of runners heading to the finish.

Ruth Anne was ready with her signs as we tracked our friends on the BAA racing app.

Erin and Ruth Anne have a very special relationship that transcends the patient/OT relationship. We cheered on friends and gave shout outs to the Spaulding Race for Rehab Team. Tom followed Erin on the map so we knew when she would be getting close. Ruth Anne spotted her halfway down Beacon Street screaming, "Erin! Erin!" jumping up and down with her sign. We knew she was struggling as many runners often do by the time they reach mile 23, especially when trying to qualify as Erin hoped. She was walking but came over to give us high fives and a big smile. She took off running down Beacon Street to the finish.

She told us later in an email that seeing us there gave her such a boost of energy. She knew what Ruth Anne overcame in her marathon of healing and the critical role she played helping Ruth

Anne regain her independence and quality of life. When she first worked with Erin in November of 2019, Ruth Anne couldn't stay awake throughout the day, manage her money or meds, or perform simple activities of living. Ruth Anne worked so hard under Erin's guidance and it was a magical moment on Marathon Monday when Ruth Anne gave Erin the boost she needed to get through the last several miles of her lifelong dream to run the Boston Marathon!

Today is the 13th anniversary of when Team McManus ran the 113th Boston Marathon.

There are always so many inspiring stories that embody the Spirit of the Marathon. After 1,099 days, the running of the Boston Marathon itself symbolized endurance, resilience, strength, patience, pacing and the ability to keep going the distance despite the challenges and heartbreak that arise.

It seems like only yesterday that I started the On The Road to Providence For Victory Programs album to document Ruth Anne and Tom's journey of training and fundraising. It started out as on the road to the Providence Marathon, but after a 15 mile training run left Tom sideways, Team McManus opted for the Half Marathon distance. They received so much support from our village and Victory Programs for their decision. When we talked with Coach Brian Simons, we talked about how the pandemic had taken a toll on everyone mind, body and soul. As we emerge from the pandemic, we all needed to honor what would be best for all Tom and Ruth Anne as runners, and for me as the marathon manager.

As you know by now, our last race-cation was in February of 2020 at Hyannis Marathon Weekend. As we crowded the ballroom and hallways, greeted each other with hugs and high fives and warmly hugged each other goodbye with "See you in Boston," we had no idea life would come to a screeching halt a few weeks later. The pandemic has been quite the journey. I know how incredibly blessed we have been through it all. Ruth Anne had to take yet another COVID-19 test for work and once again it was negative. We have all been physically healthy throughout the pandemic. There were bumps along the road exacerbated by the pandemic that took a toll on our emotional well-being but gratitude helps us to keep a perspective on how blessed and fortunate we are.

Tom and Ruth Anne trained through every kind of weather. The forecast looks amazing for Sunday. The question is how many times can I refresh the Weather Channel page set to Providence weather before Sunday. We started packing last week checking off necessities that we could pack ahead of time on our list. This race-cation has a very different feel from pre-pandemic race-cations. There is an excitement intensified by the two year hiatus since we had a running vacation. Appreciation and gratitude overflow knowing how precious life is. Our freedom to travel, stay at a hotel and gather with friends at a race weekend is no longer something we come to expect in our lives.

During an interview on Tuesday, chief medical advisor Anthony Fauci shared that the U.S. is "out of the pandemic phase" of COVID-19 as hospitalizations and cases have plummeted.

Fauci made his statement during an interview with PBS's "NewsHour" when he was asked if the nation was close to the end of the pandemic.

"We are certainly right now in this country out of the pandemic phase," Fauci said.

During an interview with The Washington Post, Fauci clarified that the global pandemic is still going on, but the U.S. is going through a transition period.

"The world is still in a pandemic. There's no doubt about that. Don't anybody get any misinterpretation of that. We are still experiencing a pandemic," Fauci said.

However, he said that the virus is no longer causing the same amount of hospitalizations and deaths that it had when omicron swept the nation over the winter.

Throughout the winter, Fauci said the U.S. was experiencing a "full-blown pandemic phase." Then, he said when cases started falling, it moved into a "deceleration" phase, and now we are transitioning to the control phase.

"The way we were months ago, we were having 900,000 cases a day, tens of thousands of hospitalizations, three thousand deaths a day," Fauci said. "The deaths went from 3,000 down to 300."

Fauci predicted we would hit a "control" stage of the pandemic by last fall, before the delta and omicron variants emerged, causing a spike in cases. Now he is saying the same, as new variants are not posing a threat.

The doctor said that omicron subvariants have started to spread, they are not impacting hospitalizations or deaths like their variant predecessor.

"Right now, we're at a low enough level that I believe that we're transitioning into endemicity. ... We're not in the full-blown explosive pandemic phase. That does not mean that the pandemic is over," Fauci said. "A pandemic means widespread infection throughout the world. ... In our country, we're transitioning into more of a controlled endemicity."

With cases declining, the nation has started to adjust to a new way of life as mask mandates, restrictions, and other COVID-19 era policies continue to be lifted. Even though mandates are becoming a thing of the past, COVID-19 is still present in our communities, and health experts continue to urge Americans to make the best choices for themselves.

During a race-cation, we would plan to take advantage of all of the hotel amenities. We decided to forego use of the swimming pool. Food service at the hotel is still limited so we will be bringing all of our breakfast needs for race day. We will look like we are going away for a week with all of our bags but that was true pre-pandemic.

When we check into the hotel, we will have come full circle from the last week of February in 2020. Once again we are able to look forward to a weekend of excitement, bib pick-ups, pre-race fueling for runners and support crew, asking people as they pass by, "You running on Sunday?", getting up at the crack of dawn on Sunday, feeling #allthefeels and heading to the start line. We are visualizing Race Weekend from start to finish with exactly how we want it to be. It's easy for gremlin thoughts, residue from having lived through the pandemic, to creep in but I keep coming back to focusing on how we all want the weekend to be and staying focused on only positive experiences.

"Good health, peace of mind, being outdoors, camaraderie - those are wonderful things that come to us when running. But for me, the real pull of running - the proverbial icing on the cake - has always been racing." ~Bill Rodgers

Whether being a runner or a spectator, the experience of a race weekend is exhilarating. It has been two years since we have been able to feel the energy and sense of community that is part of a race-cation. During the pre-Boston Marathon festivities last October, Ruth Anne planned to run the Boston Marathon in April for Spaulding Rehab. Applications would open in December. Once we had a proper diagnosis and treatment for Ruth Anne, and she was on the road to recovery, Ruth Anne fell in love with volunteering at ReVision Urban Farm. She created a birthday fundraiser for me in December of 2020 and continued fund raising for her birthday in August of 2021.

Eve Rabinowitz, the Corporate and Community Engagement Manager for Victory Programs reached out to Ruth Anne last November. She noted that she knew Ruth Anne was involved with different causes and might not have the time, but would she consider doing a Friends Feeding Friends fundraiser. Ruth Anne took a pause on running Boston and talked with Eve about running the Providence Marathon to raise money for Victory Programs and the Farm. Eve was ecstatic and set up her fundraising page with an initial goal of $3000.

Brian Simons, who I knew through Spaulding Rehab's Race for Rehab Team, was launching his new coaching business. Brian was establishing a new business and Team McManus needed a coach. In early December, we partnered with Brian and Creaky Bones Running Coaching Performance. They trained with heart, dedication, persistence and determination and race day was epic!

We drove to Providence, went to bib pick-up, and our room at the Omni Providence was ready for an early check-in. We had never been to Providence before (although we had planned a stop there on our New York road trip) and it was challenging to navigate our way around since people encouraged us to use the skywalk from the hotel to the mall. We eventually found our way to UNO Pizzeria (and found a penny along the way) despite 'Google girl" repeatedly telling us our destination was on the right which was a cement wall in the parking garage.

We were so happy to get off of our feet back in the room. We unpacked and had a long meditation/nap. We went downstairs to get bottles of sparkling water and the once quiet and subdued lobby was bustling with activity. Runners had their gear in tow and we were asking one another, "What are you running tomorrow," since there was a half and full marathon option. We were thrilled with our early check in and a room on the 3rd floor where we could hunker down away from the excitement with room service.

The beauty of the setting sun bode well for race day.

We had the alarm set to rise and shine at 5:45 to allow for plenty of time for breakfast, pre-race bathroom time (runners will appreciate the importance of that step), and walking to the starting line. I, woke up before the alarm at 5:00am watching the sun rise and getting preparations ready for Tom and Ruth Anne.

Throngs of runners lined the streets on the path to the starting line. We arrived in time to hear the start of the marathon and take pre-race photos.

"Look! There's Brian," Ruth Anne shouted. He came running over to us. I love how we're able to find people in a crowd of over 2000 runners.

Brian's presence helped to calm pre-race jitters especially for me as a spectator. We sent Tom and Ruth Anne off to the back of the pack and Brian and I waited at the start to cheer them on their 13.1 journey.

Brian helped me to get set up at the finish line while he went out to find a spot to cheer them on out on the course.

I sent out lots of great energy for Tom and Ruth Anne while reading the social media messages of cheers and prayers. I was a little unnerved when I received a text saying Ruth Anne crossed the finish at 8:04 with a course time of 2:04:43 and a pace of 9:32. Right after I received the text, Eve (who was coming down with Chief Development Office Deborah Edison to cheer on Tom and Ruth Anne at the finish) texted me asking if that was correct. I told her no worries, they just started, I did not expect to receive a text with an update and knew I just had to trust in their training and of course the Divine.

What a very pleasant surprise to receive a text with an update at the 10K letting me know that Tom and Ruth Anne were running a 14:46 minute/mile pace. I immediately texted Brian who responded with, "Perfect. I found a great spot at Mile 11."

I was getting a little anxious as I calculated the pace and how far they had to go to Mile 11 (never a good idea) and asked Brian if he saw them. "Not yet," he replied, "Soon." He let me know that they were back on the roads after Mile 11 with smiles and were slowed down by porta-potty stops but reassured me they were looking strong. "They're walking," he added letting me know that they slowed their pace. They had planned to do a run/walk interval. By mile 11, Tom was feeling the miles and they lengthened the walk intervals to ensure a strong finish.

Eve texted me to say they arrived but she couldn't find me. The crowd of spectators had grown thick by then as runners began to cross the finish line. "I'm wearing the red Victory Programs shirt," she texted and within a minute we found each other. I was so grateful that I did not have to wait alone during those last 2.1 miles. Another friend texted that they were on their way but were having trouble parking. "Have they crossed yet?" Karen asked. A moment before I received her text, Ruth Anne texted me with, "One mile to go." The text came sooner than I expected!

We all had our cameras ready to capture the epic moment. Brian was able to capture the announcement of them crossing the finish line on video. I wasn't sure if my video even came out because I was so overcome with emotion but it did, capturing an epic moment in the life of Team McManus and the post-pandemic world. I love how Tom and Ruth Anne high-fived and embraced each other. Tom and Ruth Anne made their way over to us. It was as though the runners and spectators around us faded into the background while Tom, Ruth Anne, Eve, Deborah, Brian, Karen and her husband Chris excitedly talked with each other. Karen said this was such a great opportunity to check off seeing Tom and me. We were about to get together before the pandemic. Karen said she has a list of people on her "we were planning to get together list and then the pandemic happened."

Deborah and Eve regaled us with gratitude and compliments and yet Ruth Anne thanked them for this amazing opportunity.

As a thank you gift, they presented us with beautiful track jackets embroidered with the Victory Programs logo. Our hearts overflowed with love, gratitude, joy, excitement for the accomplishment of running a half marathon and exhilaration for an incredibly successful fundraising campaign.

Ruth Anne said that crossing that finish line would be the beginning of a new season in her life.

Every finish line is a starting line! Ruth Anne is so excited to explore career possibilities in this next season of her life. Tom feels vibrant and energized by being able to run a half marathon at age 70. A year ago, Tom felt 'old' but he realized he still had a LOT of life left in him. He left his job where he was under appreciated and experienced age discrimination and is now in an extremely successful contract role. Training for this race gave him that extra boost he needed to feel healthy and younger than his biological age. He enters a new season in his life with great anticipation of perhaps winning his age group (he came in 7/8) and enjoying these later years of his life.

I was transformed through their journey and being a part of the racing scene again. We are emerging from the pandemic into the light stronger and more resilient than before the pandemic began. I am celebrating 15 years of healing this month. On 5/25/2007, I set off on a new season of my life taking a leap of faith leaving behind my award-winning social work career to heal my life.

It's a time of wondrous and wonderful happenings that was reflected in conversations overheard after the race. One marathoner said, "We really needed this!"

On our way back to the hotel, we found another penny.

We enjoyed a post-race celebration meal with Tom and Ruth Anne proudly wearing their medals. Throngs of runners at The Cheesecake Factory congratulated each other and greeted each other with "How did you do?" It's been two years since we've had this kind of experience and my heart and soul overflowed with gratitude that we could have this experience again.

As for Coach Brian, he posted this on Facebook:

I am so inspired by them! It was so awesome to see their hard work and my coaching business notch its first finish!

It took a few days to process how amazing Sunday was as a coach!

I am so proud of my athletes! They did it! My clients crushed their half marathon in Providence this past weekend! A 20 minute PR! Their diligence and dedication paid off! I'm so grateful to have had the opportunity to create their training plans, adjust them as needed, and help them enjoy the process and progress!
On to the next race and goal!
#halfmarathon #runcoach #movethosebones #creakybonesrcp

Indeed -- every finish line is a starting line as we go into the light emerging from the pandemic.

"Almost everything will work again if you unplug it for a few minutes ... even you." ~Anne Lamott

Last week, Team McManus knew we needed to have a daycation; a day where we unplug, do something different for cross training and treat ourselves well with dining out for breakfast, lunch and dinner. We had not been to Falmouth, our happy place, since Memorial Day of 2021. With Tom and Ruth Anne training and fundraising, and Tom doing contract work, we didn't see our way to having more time than a few days in Hyannis celebrating the twins' 35th birthday in August. We knew it was vital for our mental and physical well-being.

"I don't know if I want to swim in the ocean if we aren't going to have any place to change," Ruth Anne said. "I'd love to get into a pool before summer is over."

I'd been thinking about this quandary and toyed with the idea of getting a room at The Admiralty Inn and Suites where we stayed for years. There is usually a two night minimum stay for Labor Day Weekend on Cape Cod. I checked their website and it looked as though there was a room available for Sunday night. I didn't give it more thought until last Thursday when Ruth Anne expressed concerns about being in our 'crusty' bathing suits all day.

"Hello Admiralty Inn and Suites."

"Hi I was wondering if you have a minimum night stay for this weekend."

"I'm sorry but we're booked for the weekend."

"Oh I thought I saw a room available for Sunday night on the website."

"I'm sorry. I misunderstood you. When you said weekend..."

258

"Oh no it's my fault. I should have been more specific. With whom am I speaking? Is this Eric?"

"Yes it is. Whose this?"

I gave him my name and he said, "Well let me get you set up with a great room. We've recently renovated the property and I'd love for you to see the new courtyard room. ... Let me get you in for a great rate."

I explained that we weren't going to stay overnight but wanted to use the property's amenities and to shower and change after beach and pool time. "Absolutely," he said. "We look forward to welcoming you back!"

We left very early Sunday morning to avoid traffic. Everyone says how you feel the magic of stress release driving over the Bridge to 'The Cape'. We agreed that we would take pictures but not post on Facebook or be on line for the entire day.

Our first stop was Crabapples, our favorite breakfast place in Falmouth. We checked out The Admiralty Inn and let the front desk staff know that we knew our room wouldn't be ready, but Eric let us know that we could use the pool. "Absolutely," she said and added, "Let me have your phone number so I can call you when the room is ready."

There was a family that had taken over a section of the pool deck playing loud music. We didn't want to disturb them or ourselves and headed for the beach. We spent the entire morning on the beach. I meditated, read, put my toes in the water and took videos to enjoy when winter returns to New England. Tom rested, read and meditated. Ruth Anne frolicked in the waves and swam feeling unbridled joy free from the constraints of a training plan feeling the healing power of sun and sea. She put down beach towels and fell asleep to the sounds of the waves.

When lunchtime came, we were going to go to Shipwrecked but the Universe had other plans. There was a long line along with the smell of deep fried food. We dried off and headed to Main Street. There were long lines at most places. "Why don't we go to the Quarterdeck Restaurant?" I suggested to Tom and Ruth Anne. During the pandemic we wouldn't have dared to venture inside of a crowded bar and restaurant but since COVID-19 is now considered endemic, we were delighted to get a lovely table with wonderful service.

It was Ruth Anne's first visit to The Quarterdeck restaurant and we reminisced about Cape Cod Marathon Weekend when we met Tommy Leonard. We all enjoyed reminiscing about previous trips to Falmouth as a family. After we finished lunch we had a big question to ask... Do we or don't we?

We did! We got ice cream from Ben and Bill's, an indie owned ice cream shop that fortunately survived the pandemic. What a treat to walk up and down the bustling sidewalk and shops of Main Street with barely a trace of the pandemic.

It was time to head back to the Admiralty Inn for swimming, relaxation, more meditation and showers. Our Courtyard Room opened up to the pool area and we had a private patio. Ruth Anne and I went into the pool to swim and stretch while Tom rested in the room since he was our designated driver.

What a treat to have a place to shower, change and relax after a day of fun in the sun.

The last time we were at The Flying Bridge, Memorial Day of 2021, we couldn't stay for dinner. It was a rainy day and the plastic enclosure from the winter was still in place. The scent of hand sanitizer, seeing a sea of empty tables and weary wait staff left us feeling sad wondering if we would ever be able to return to our beloved restaurant on beautiful Falmouth Harbor.

There was a line out the door but only a 20 minute wait. We saw members of a wedding party arrive. It was a perfect end of summer evening. We took a walk while we waited to receive the text that our table was ready. Waitstaff were taking a break outside and Tom asked them how their summer was. They said it was their best season ever! Drinks and plates overflowing with the traditional Flying Bridge fare were served with flair and joy. Friends and families' conversations were animated as laughter echoed throughout the harbor. Patrons were packed close together. There was a rhythm and ease to the service despite the number of customers eager to enjoy their drinks and food.

We heard a spontaneous eruption of applause as the bride and groom walked along the harbor walk to have their photos taken. There was so much to celebrate beyond a wedding and end of summer. Celebration for the end of the pandemic was palpable.

As we drove across the bridge heading home, I felt recharged and renewed ready to begin a new season. I reflected on the stark contrast between the summer of 2021 and Labor Day 2022. Ruth Anne and Tom are training for three half marathons. At the end of our Hyannis vacation, Ruth Anne set a new running and fundraising goal. We are excited for so many job prospects open to her. Tom transitions from contract work to employee. When he took his leap of faith leaving Boston College, we knew we would land on our feet as we always have but couldn't possibly have imagined he would be hired for a job he loves with an incredible manager and co-workers who truly value him as a professional and as a person. My opportunities to share my incredible journey and powerful message of healing, hope and possibilities continue to flow into my life. Autumn is going to be filled with beautiful new beginnings.

Final Reflections

A Pot Luck Brunch   September 11, 2022

The President of L Street Running Club posted on Facebook that there would be a 5K or a 5 mile run happening on September 11, followed by a Pot Luck Brunch. We'd meet by the beach in South Boston. Despite being deep in training for three half marathons and needing to get up early on a Sunday morning, our one day to 'sleep in,' we knew how vital it was to see our friends again. The last time we were with our running family, we had masks and proof of vaccination at packet stuffing in October. On March 8, 2020, we hosted a water stop for L Street. It would be the last time we greeted each other with maskless faces, hugs and sweat.

There was a spread of bagels, fruit, pastries, coffee and water bottles lovingly set out by the executives of our Club. We added our bagels, lox and cream cheese to the 'pot' as we embraced members returning from their runs. Although the day was overcast, the love among us shined brightly.

"This is quite a difference from the last time we saw each other at packet stuffing," I said to Nancy, one of our close friends in the Club.

"And how about before that at the water stop?" she added. "It's a changed world now isn't it? So much has happened."

The gathering was one of those 'time warp' moments where it seemed as though nothing and yet everything changed since we last gathered together. One of our dear friends is heading to Berlin to run the Berlin Marathon. She shared her woes about getting her trip scheduled; remnants of a post-pandemic world with staffing shortages and skyrocketing fuel costs.

What a blessing to be able to literally break bread together and to catch up on what was happening in each other's lives. The conversation flowed as easily as the ebb and flow of the tide. Excitement for upcoming events both in personal lives and on the running scene were amplified by the pause in our lives since the pandemic. With the help of social media, we were able to maintain and strengthen the connections we share as running family. On the anniversary of 9/11, a day that was overwhelmed with darkness, we gathered to share our love and our light remembering our incredible strength and resilience. Whatever the challenge, on the roads or in life, we go the distance, together, into the light.

Into the Light

In winter's darkness
as pandemic "rages" on
turning inward
rhythm of my beating heart
radiates warmth
beaming Love to heal weary world
harping on darkness.
Love beams spark hope
harbingers of lightness and ease
focus on Source if you please
gratitude flows for miracles on horizon
be in the flow
this too shall pass.
Let burdens be lifted
shift to a new perspective
bright and bold
declaring all is well
confidently
deftly
running into the light.

References

Tara Brach   www.tarabrach.com

Amy Cuddy   www.amycuddy.com

Dr. Joe Dispenza www.drjoedispenza.com

Victor Frankl https://viktorfranklamerica.com/viktor-frankl-bio/

Dr. David R. Hamilton www.drdavidhamilton.com

Dr. Peter Levine https://www.somaticexperiencing.com/about-peter

Lin-Manuel Miranda   https://www.linmanuel.com/

Bernie Siegel, MD   www.berniesiegelmd.com

Brian Simons www.creakybonesrcp.com

Desmond Tutu https://theelders.org/profile/desmond-tutu

About the Author

Mary McManus, motivational speaker, critically acclaimed author and poet, 2009 Boston Marathon finisher, and polio and trauma survivor has a remarkable story of resilience, healing, hope and possibilities. She is celebrating 15 years of healing after the diagnosis of Post-Polio Syndrome, a progressive neuromuscular disease!

Mary contracted paralytic polio in one of the last polio epidemics in the United States. She endured years of abuse at the hands of family members from the age of 8 until 17 when her father ended his life. She managed to become High School Valedictorian and was elected to Alpha Sigma Nu, the Jesuit Honor Society when she received her MSW from Boston College.

At the age of 53 years old, her life came to a screeching halt. She was at the height of her award-winning career as a social worker at the Boston VA Outpatient Clinic having received awards from the Blinded Veterans Association, the Ex-POW's, Employee of the Month and Social Worker of the Year. She was diagnosed with Post-Polio Syndrome, a progressive neuromuscular disease and was told to prepare to spend the rest of her life in a wheelchair. She was three years shy of being eligible for retirement.

Mary refused to take the diagnosis sitting down. Her pen became her divining rod for healing harnessing the power of the mind/body connection through poetry. She embarked on a journey that took her from taking a leap of faith, leaving behind her career as a VA social worker, to the finish line of the 2009 Boston Marathon, and many adventures as a woman transformed through the sport of running. Out of the rubble of her past, Mary dug deep to discover the treasure of who she was always meant to be. Her Spirit shines with brilliant resilience as she conquered every challenge going the distance on the roads and in her life.

Mary is the author of the critically acclaimed, "Hope is a Garden: Poems and Essays From the 2020 Pandemic", "Feel the Heal: An

Anthology of Poems to Heal Your Life," and her Trilogy of Transformation that chronicles her health and wellness journey. Mary has shared her story on many podcasts and radio shows, including the award-winning Exceptional Women radio show. Mary was featured on Boston's Channel 7 after her inspiring Boston Marathon run, is featured on the Heal Documentary website and featured in best-selling author Dr. David Hamilton's book, "The Tenth Anniversary Edition of How Your Mind Can Heal Your Body." Recently, Mary was the guest on the All Things Rex Worldwide Show sponsored by the Los Angeles Tribune.

Mary holds a BS in Communications from Boston University, an MSW from Boston College and many fond memories of her veterans and their families who blessed her life when she worked at the VA. She lives in Chestnut Hill Massachusetts with her husband, Tom of 45 years, and their lovely cat Jamie. They are the proud parents of 35 year old twins, Ruth Anne and her brother Autumn.